TWAYNE'S WORLD LEADERS SERIES

EDITORS OF THIS VOLUME

Arthur W. Brown

Baruch College, The City University of New York

and

Thomas S. Knight

Adelphi University

Franklin D. Roosevelt

Franklin D. Roosevelt

Franklin D. Roosevelt:

The Contribution of the New Deal to American Political Thought and Practice

MORTON J. FRISCH

TWAYNE PUBLISHERS
A DIVISION OF G. K. HALL & CO., BOSTON

Library of Congress Cataloging in Publication Data

Frisch, Morton J.
Franklin D. Roosevelt; the contribution of the New Deal to American political thought and practice.

(Twayne's world leaders series)
Bibliography: p. 158–62.
1. United States—Politics and government—1933–1945.
2. Roosevelt, Franklin Delano, Pres. U. S., 1882–1945.
E806.F74 320.9′73′0917 [B] 74-16425
ISBN 0–8057–3708–1 2-27-76

MANUFACTURED IN THE UNITED STATES OF AMERICA

For Joelyn

* * *

The greatness of America is grounded in principles.

Franklin D. Roosevelt, Campaign Address,
November 5, 1932.

Contents

About the Author

Morton J. Frisch is Professor of Political Science at Northern Illinois University. He was on the faculty of the College of William and Mary from 1953–64 and Fulbright Professor of Political Science at the University of Stockholm in 1963–64. He is co-author and co-editor of *The Thirties: A Reconsideration in the Light of the American Political Tradition* (1968) and *American Political Thought: The Philosophic Dimension of American Statesmanship* (1971) and co-editor of *The Political Thought of American Statesmen: Selected Writings and Speeches* (1973).

Prefatory Note

In the course of this study (Chapter 4), I found it necessary to consider Richard Hofstadter's critique of Roosevelt in his book *The American Political Tradition.* Appendix 1 contains an exposition of the point of view in the light of which that criticism was made.

Appendix 2 deals with the question of whether a democratic political theory has a place in American political life. Daniel J. Boorstin's argument that the absence of a democratic political theory constitutes the genius of American politics is examined there.

Acknowledgments

Grateful acknowledgment is made to the University of Chicago Press for permission to use revised versions of essays that originally appeared in the January, 1961, and October, 1963, issues of *Ethics*; to the editors of the *Journal of Politics* for permission to use essays that appeared in the May, 1963, and August, 1967, issues; and to the Northern Illinois University Press for permission to use a revised version of my essay from *The Thirties* published in 1968.

I would like to express my appreciation to Professor Martin Diamond of Northern Illinois University and especially to Professor Richard G. Stevens of Rockford College for the encouragement and criticism they gave me during the course of my Roosevelt study.

Chronology

1882 Born on January 3 at Hyde Park, New York, a fifth cousin of Theodore Roosevelt.

1896–1900 Attended Groton School and graduated in 1900.

1900–1904 Studied at Harvard College and graduated in 1904.

1904–1907 Studied at the Columbia University Law School.

1905 Married on March 17 to Anna Eleanor Roosevelt.

1907 Admitted to the New York State bar.

1910–1913 Served as a member of the New York State Senate.

1913–1920 Served as Assistant Secretary of the Navy under Josephus Daniels.

1920 Nominated as Democratic vice-presidential candidate with James M. Cox.

1921 Struck by paralytic poliomyelitis at Campobello, New Brunswick.

1924–1928 Nominated Al Smith twice for the presidential candidacy of the Democratic party.

1927 Established the Warm Springs Foundation, a nonprofit organization for the care of polio victims.

1929–1933 Served as governor of New York for two terms.

1933–1945 Served as 32nd President of the United States, being reelected for four terms.

1933 Established diplomatic relations with the government of the Soviet Union.

The Hundred Days, a special session of Congress lasting from March 9 to June 16 in which the New Deal's initial recovery and reform laws were submitted for congressional approval.

1935 Inaugurated the Good Neighbor Policy toward Latin American nations.

1937 Attempted to "pack" the United States Supreme Court.

1938 Attempted to "purge" recalcitrant Democratic congressmen in the party primaries.

1939– Worked to reverse previous neutrality policy of the

1941 United States and inaugurate Lend-Lease aid to Great Britain and the Soviet Union.

1941 Signed the Atlantic Charter with Winston Churchill.

1943 Attended Casablanca and Teheran conferences, meeting at the first with Churchill and at the second with Churchill and Stalin.

1945 Attended the Yalta Conference, meeting with Churchill and Stalin.
Died on April 12 at Warm Springs, Georgia.

CHAPTER 1

Roosevelt's Political Career

FRANKLIN D. Roosevelt, four times elected President of the United States, was in direct line of descent from Claes Martenszen Van Roosevelt, who emigrated from Holland to New Amsterdam in the early seventeenth century. The latter's only surviving son, Nicholas, dropped the "Van," calling himself simply Roosevelt, and was the first to use that name in America. Whatever the formative influences were on the young Franklin Roosevelt, surely Endicott Peabody, headmaster of the Groton School, Theodore Roosevelt, and Woodrow Wilson must be taken into account. Roosevelt knew Theodore Roosevelt, his own cousin, and hence was not unfamiliar with what the true conservative was like. His own aristocratic upbringing, moreover, contributed to that awareness.

There were four stages in Roosevelt's political education prior to his election to the presidency: his state senate experience, 1910–1912; his assistant secretaryship of the navy, 1913–1920; his nomination and campaign for the vice-presidency in 1920; and his two terms as governor of New York State, 1929–1932. At each stage of his early political career he was thinking about the presidency, stimulated no doubt by the fact that his cousin Theodore had held that office. He consciously tried to avoid the gubernatorial nomination in New York in 1928, assuming that he would move into the national political limelight too quickly and thus endanger the eventual possibility of a presidential nomination. There was no lack of political ambition in Franklin Roosevelt.

Roosevelt went to Groton, Harvard, the Columbia University Law School, and then into politics. He made bossism versus clean government the issue of his campaign for the New York State Senate in 1910, running as a Democrat; and his victory in that election was part of a national trend. Woodrow Wilson won the governorship of New Jersey that same year. Roosevelt's most noteworthy actions in the New York assembly were his opposition to the dominance of Tammany Hall, leading the Democratic insurgents to block the nomination of William F. Sheehan, the choice of Boss Murphy, and his support for the direct election of United States senators. He appeared as a kind of Progressive in his legislative activities, supporting the conservation of national resources, the woman suffrage amendment, municipal home rule, direct primaries for party nominations, and some forms of social reform legislation. But he was not a strong supporter of labor reform legislation, his record on that being somewhat mixed.

Roosevelt's support of Woodrow Wilson for the presidency in 1912, not to mention the attention he received as leader of the anti-Tammany insurgents in the New York State Senate, earned him the assistant secretaryship of the navy under Josephus Daniels. Daniels was the only administrative superior Roosevelt ever had in his entire political career, and he was at odds with the secretary a good part of the time. There was, however, a good deal of give and take between them. In 1914, just four years after entering political life, Roosevelt made an attempt to secure the Democratic nomination for United States senator from New York but he was blocked by Tammany. It was the only defeat of his political career and resulted from his underestimating Tammany's resourcefulness. His job in the Navy Department continued, and his political administration of naval affairs during World War I afforded him kinds of responsibilities that an assistant secretary would not ordinarily assume. He also delivered a number of speeches, while in that position, advocating America's entrance into the League of Nations.

In 1920 Roosevelt was nominated by the Democratic party as its vice-presidential candidate to run on the national ticket with James M. Cox of Ohio. In contrast to Cox, Roosevelt was closely identified with the Wilson administration. Cox and Roosevelt decided to campaign largely on the League of Nations issue, despite their realization that it was potentially dangerous; their campaign could therefore be interpreted as a principled campaign. The Democrats were defeated by Harding by over seven million votes, a defeat which could be considered an endorsement of isolationism.

In August, 1921, Roosevelt was severely stricken with

poliomyelitis at Campobello Island off the coast of New Brunswick. There seems to be a myth current that, as a result of that illness, which had paralyzed his legs, Roosevelt underwent a profound transformation in character, from superciliousness to humanitarianism, and that he became the person we remember from his presidential years. While Roosevelt surely matured as a result of his political experiences, it would be difficult to say that his illness had any substantial effect on his character or outlook. His refusal to retire from politics, in spite of his illness, can be best understood as another example of his hard-driving ambition and will.

Roosevelt's presidential nominating speeches for Al Smith in the 1924 and 1928 Democratic conventions set the stage for his own entrance into the corridors of power. In 1928, moreover, he was nominated by acclamation as the Democratic party's choice for governor of New York against his own previous intentions, for to run for office in that year might have meant going down to defeat with a Catholic presidential candidate. Roosevelt won the governorship by 25,000 votes despite the fact that Smith failed to carry the state against Herbert Hoover. Roosevelt was reelected in 1930 by a plurality of 725,000 votes. As governor of New York, he gained national prominence. In his attempt to find ways of dealing with the deepening depression crisis, his second-term gubernatorial program anticipated many of his later New Deal programs in the presidency. That program included labor legislation, old-age pensions, unemployment insurance, and public utility regulation. Roosevelt's two terms as governor of New York were clearly the indispensable preparation for his assumption of the presidency. They enabled him to achieve a truly national image, provided the necessary administrative experience in managing the affairs of the largest state in the nation, and provided that necessary party experience for the national political scene into which he was soon to move. When Jim Farley, at a later time, wanted the presidential nomination virtually handed to him as a matter of right, Roosevelt urged him to first run for governor of New York, a course he refused to follow. This refusal merely confirmed what Roosevelt had already believed, namely, that anyone who was unwilling to run for office on the state level was not made of presidential timber. The governorship of New York State was truly a preparation for the presidency.

Once Roosevelt was reelected governor of New York by

a large majority, he became the conspicuous candidate for the Democratic presidential nomination, despite all the hard opposition to that nomination in the convention itself. It was relatively easy to block a leading contender for the nomination since a two-thirds vote in the convention was required. Roosevelt had a majority of the delegates, but he could have been blocked by a combination of Garner and Smith forces. The turning point in the convention was Roosevelt's offer of the vice-presidency, through Jim Farley, to John Nance Garner of Texas, the acceptance of which required Garner to throw his support to FDR. After that deal was consummated, the Roosevelt bandwagon could not be stopped. Considering the opposition, it is difficult to see how the Roosevelt nomination could have been successfully managed without Farley's skillful bargaining at the convention. In the 1932 election, Roosevelt received 22,860,000 popular and 472 electoral votes to Hoover's 15,720,000 popular and 59 electoral votes, despite Hoover's admonition that a Roosevelt victory would mean that grass would soon be growing in the streets.

The initial actions of the new administration, a kind of prelude to the New Deal itself, consisted of a wide array of measures designed to inspire confidence in the sagging American economy. In 1933, industrial production in the country was down by 56 percent from the 1923–1925 level. This initial legislative program was enacted in approximately the first one hundred days of the new administration and represented Roosevelt's effort to provide quick recovery for all the diverse groupings in the economy and eliminate some of the causes of the depression. But the main emphasis was on recovery, including measures creating the National Recovery Administration, the Agricultural Adjustment Administration, the Reconstruction Finance Corporation, and the Tennessee Valley Authority.

The bulk of Roosevelt's efforts during the New Deal period of his presidency were given over to getting laws on the statute books for regulating the national economy, establishing welfare programs, and strengthening and reshaping the national administration. Among the greatest innovations introduced by New Deal legislation were the Social Security Act, the Fair Labor Standards Act, the National Labor Relations Act, and the Government Reorganization Act. Indeed, it would be no exaggeration to say that Roosevelt's New Deal so completely set the tone for the politics of succeeding generations that we still think and act largely within the broad lines of the liberal doctrines articulated during that period. The Democratic party of the present day, profoundly influenced by the liberal doctrines of which Roosevelt was the chief architect, has been unable to move beyond the horizons of that liberalism.

Roosevelt's victory over Alfred M. Landon in 1936 was 27,750,000 popular and 523 electoral votes to 16,680,000 popular and 8 electoral votes (those of Maine and Vermont), the most overwhelming electoral victory since the reelection of James Monroe in 1828. That election was the first real test of Roosevelt's political strength. The decline in the Socialist vote was staggering, for it had dropped from 881,000 in 1932 to 187,000 in 1936, even though six million more Americans had cast their votes. Norman Thomas, the Socialist party leader, admitted that FDR and his New Deal had contributed more to the destruction of that party's viability in America than had any other single factor.

There were three climactic moments in Roosevelt's domestic career as President: his struggle with the Supreme Court from 1935 to 1937, culminating in the court-packing controversy; his attempt to purge Democratic congressmen in the 1938 party primaries; and the opposition to his third-term nomination in 1940. Both domestic and foreign policy considerations were involved in his decision to run for a third term; hence, that controversy provides a link between the domestic and foreign policy phases of his presidential career.

The court-packing bill, which FDR presented to the Congress shortly after his overwhelming second-term victory, provoked one of the bitterest constitutional debates in American history. The primary purpose of that bill was to get some Roosevelt appointees on the Supreme Court, that is, to alter the balance of power between liberal and conservative justices on that Court and hence the Court's decisions. The Court's actions in 1935 and 1936 in striking down many crucial pieces of New Deal legislation threatened the virtual extinction of the New Deal program. Charles Evans Hughes presided over the most serious crisis in the Supreme Court's history. He presided over that Court's decision that the New Deal did not square with the Constitution, as well as over a dramatic reversal of that same decision in 1937.

The Hughes Court employed the distinction between direct

and indirect effects on interstate commerce, and hence a narrow interpretation of the commerce clause, especially in the Schechter decision nullifying the NRA, as one of the principal means of keeping the national government out of the economic marketplace. Roosevelt argued for a broader interpretation of the commerce clause which would allow it to be used to regulate all the interrelated elements of the nation's economy. His famous "horse and buggy" press conference, following the Schechter decision in 1935, may have swung public opinion behind the President; but it had no effect whatsoever on the decisions of the Supreme Court itself. Following the court-packing proposal in early 1937, however, a resignation from the Court and a number of critical decisions reflecting a more tolerant attitude toward New Deal welfare and regulatory legislation provided for the transition from the Hughes Court to the Roosevelt Court. But this is not to suggest that Roosevelt's court-packing proposal, which failed to secure congressional approval, convinced the Hughes Court or members of that Court to shift from their previous position.

The charge has often been made that Roosevelt was not a party leader but a party dictator, which suggests that he was using the Democratic party for merely partisan rather than national purposes. James Farley characterizes Roosevelt's attempt to "purge" the Democratic party of some of its more dissident elements in the 1938 primaries as an attempt to establish a personal party. Politically, FDR tried to take revenge, it is true, for the refusal of dissident Democratic senators to support major New Deal bills, including his court-packing plan. Samuel Rosenman points out that "the purge had its birth in Roosevelt's personal resentment at the two major legislative defeats dealt him by members of his own party—the defeat of the Supreme Court plan in the spring and summer of 1937; and the defeat of two other pieces of legislation in the Extraordinary Session in the fall of 1937: the wages and hours bill and the administration reorganization bill."[1]

Roosevelt did not succeed in cleansing the party of its most dissident elements in 1938, and in that sense the purge was a failure. The purge, however, did not disclose its real consequences for many years thereafter, for Roosevelt impressed a new spirit on the Democratic party. But in order to do that he had to appeal to liberal principles. The liberal principles embodied in the New Deal were so little ingrained in the rank and file of the Democratic party in 1937–1938 that it was difficult to tell what the party stood for, especially in view of the widespread cleavage between the New Deal and conservative Democrats. Before the party primaries in 1938, the Democratic party was by no means fixed in the liberal mold FDR cast upon it as a result of that primary struggle. Therefore, the purge did have a positive effect, insofar as establishing the principled basis of that party is concerned.

The supreme action of Roosevelt's political career, the action whereby he provided for the perpetuation of the massive accomplishments of the New Deal as well as for America's intervention in the European war, was his willingness to break with the two-term tradition, a tradition that he was never committed to as a matter of principle. The third-term issue provided the transition from reformism to internationalism, for in that decision were reflected FDR's hopes for the future in the realm of domestic policy and his fears for the future in the realm of foreign policy. Although his decision to run was partly conditioned by his feeling that he had not had a chance to complete the Roosevelt Revolution in his second term, foreign policy issues loomed large in that decision. Prior to 1938, he dealt almost exclusively with domestic problems. But the Munich crisis in August of that year called for a reassessment of priorities in Roosevelt's thinking. Indicative of that reassessment, he announced, in his annual message to Congress in January, 1939, that the order of emphasis between domestic and foreign policy was to be reversed: henceforth his administration would seek no new domestic reforms and would place its primary emphasis on the achievement of collective security.

Norman Thomas accused FDR in 1940 of instituting the first peacetime draft in the nation's history because of the sense of personal power it gave him. The letter the President wrote in answer to that charge is one of the most remarkable documents of his entire political correspondence:

> You and I may perhaps disagree as to the danger to the United States—but we can at least give each other credit for the honesty that lies behind our opinions. Frankly, I am greatly fearful for the safety of this country over a period of years, because I think that the tendency of the present victorious dictatorships is to segregate us and surround us to such an extent that we will become vulnerable

to a final attack when they get ready to make it.... With a sincerity and an honesty equal to yours, I believe that we ought this Autumn to take some kind of action which will better prepare Americans by selection and training for national defense than we have ever done before.[2]

By a closer margin than ever before, Roosevelt defeated his most formidable candidate for the presidency, Wendell L. Willkie, by 27,240,000 popular and 449 electoral votes to 22,300,000 popular and 82 electoral votes. Against the opposition of conservative elements within the party, Roosevelt insisted that Henry A. Wallace be his running mate, replacing Garner.

The high points of the foreign policy phase of Roosevelt's presidential career were the Atlantic Charter meeting between Roosevelt and Churchill and the two great wartime conferences among Roosevelt, Churchill, and Stalin, the Teheran and Yalta conferences. Prior to the Atlantic meeting, Roosevelt was busily engaged in influencing or redirecting public opinion on the question of American neutrality toward the European war and in sending economic-military aid (after March, 1941) to Great Britain. After the German attack on the Soviet Union, he extended that aid to the Russians.

Roosevelt met with Winston Churchill, the British prime minister, at sea off the coast of Newfoundland in August, 1941, prior to the Japanese attack on Pearl Harbor. That meeting produced the most compelling statement of the war. The Atlantic Charter, with its statement of the Four Freedoms, which ironically did not even exist as a formal document, has become, on the level of abstraction, the most revolutionary document of our time; for it has inspired a sense of hope in the future that no pronouncement of the international communist movement has ever been able to achieve. The Teheran Conference in November, 1943, the first meeting among Roosevelt, Churchill, and Stalin, included some discussion of the special privileges the Soviet Union would receive in the Far East, presumably in return for its eventual participation in the Japanese war; preliminary discussion of a postwar international organization; and a discussion of the future boundaries of the Polish state, not to mention the character of that regime. Poland's fate as a Soviet satellite was anticipated at Teheran and consummated by Churchill and Stalin at the Moscow Conference in October, 1944. Only in August, 1973, through the release of previously secret papers in London, was it definitely established that Churchill agreed to the Soviet domination of Poland in October, 1944, in exchange for their recognition of British interests in the Mediterranean and the Far East.[3]

Roosevelt ran for a fourth term against Governor Thomas E. Dewey of New York, after having agreed to replace Henry A. Wallace with Harry S. Truman as his running mate. That campaign was characterized by the virtual absence of political campaigning by Roosevelt. He won by 26,600,000 popular and 432 electoral votes to 22,000,000 popular and 49 electoral votes for Dewey. After his death, those people in the 1947 Congress who were infuriated at FDR's four elections seized their opportunity to introduce and pass their two-term amendment. It was ratified in 1951.

At the Yalta Conference, in January-February, 1945, the last wartime meetings among Roosevelt, Churchill, and Stalin, a strenuous effort was made toward defining the peace. Crucial decisions were made concerning the character of the future international organization (including the whole question of trusteeships); the division and occupation of Germany after its imminent surrender; the character of the provisional Polish regime (already a foregone conclusion given Churchill's capitulation to Stalin) and of eastern European ex-Axis satellite regimes in general; and a secret understanding between Roosevelt and Stalin on concessions in Manchuria to the Soviet Union in return for its agreement to enter the Japanese war.

We are told that, in this culminating moment of his career, Roosevelt gave no clear, real guidance to the Western Allies, and submitted with complacency to Stalin's demands, especially in the Far East. But Roosevelt, in spite of all the postwar talk about concessions he made to the Russians at Yalta, in advancing the cause of the United Nations, not to mention the Declaration of Liberated Europe, imposed his will, as it were, on the aristocratic Churchill and the tyrannical Stalin. The Declaration of Liberated Europe, which emerged from that conference, was in effect a written guarantee made by Stalin that the Eastern European countries liberated from Nazi domination would have democratic elections and hence be able to determine the character of their postwar regimes. That declaration was the result of an effort on Roosevelt's part to counteract the sphere-of-influence agreements made between

Churchill and Stalin in two previous meetings in 1944, which had attempted to establish their respective spheres of influence on the European continent, and to some extent in the Far East. While the declaration was not effective insofar as the Soviet takeover in Eastern Europe was concerned (for Soviet forces were already occupying most of these territories at the time of Yalta), it served to underscore the illegality of that takeover and thus establish a basis for criticism of or an opposition to Soviet postwar imperialism.

Soon after Yalta, on April 12, 1945, Roosevelt died of a massive cerebral hemorrhage, at a time when relations between the United States and the Soviet Union were in a state of deterioration, and when the lines of the Cold War were already beginning to take shape.

CHAPTER 2

The Problem of Roosevelt's Statesmanship

ONE of the outstanding accomplishments of Roosevelt the statesman was his successful course of educating the American people in the uses of democracy, accompanied by practical examples of the doctrines he was teaching. In 1933 there were few books and no national precedents for the philosophy or legislation that came to be known as the New Deal. He had to write his own books in the form of speeches and messages, and then create the precedents himself to carry them out.

Samuel I. Rosenman, 1952

Any study of the political course of Franklin D. Roosevelt must have as its chief concern the contribution of Roosevelt's "New Deal" to both the thought and practice of American politics. The chief contention of this study is that the contribution of the New Deal to American political thought is quite as great as its place in American political practice. We mean here to uncover and explain the outline and character of that thought and show its coherent relation to that practice. We mean to show that the practice follows from the thought and thus to counter the claim, made now with increasing self-assurance, that the thought was a kind of "rationalization" for the practice. Though we do not end there, we *begin* by listening attentively to what Franklin D. Roosevelt said.

FDR managed political life in America more effectively than any other twentieth-century leader has done; for, more than anyone else, he came to grips with the problem of the class struggle, arguing that economic freedom is an essential part of political freedom. That the American people were able to withstand the shock of an unparalleled depression and that their concern for their well-being did not deteriorate into despair was, in large measure, due to the sobriety and restrained character of Roosevelt's statesmanship. That sobriety and restraint were as much a part of the action of the New Deal as the major pieces of New Deal legislation. The reconstruction of that statesmanship should make it possible to discover the principle or principles of action which were implicit in the practical political arguments and positions he adopted in over a decade of political activity in the White House.

Raymond Moley writes, in his recent book on the First New Deal, that those, including himself, who participated in the Brains Trust were too busy for mature reflection or to create a system or an overall pattern. Too often, he says, a philosophy is created long after the facts upon which it is based have ceased to exist.[1] But as Professor Harry Jaffa has pointed out,

> The way in which events appear to those who are engaged in shaping them is not necessarily the final viewpoint from which one discerns the broad patterns which exist in political history. The fact that the larger perspective is invisible while the actions are being engaged in doesn't prove that there are no broad patterns which may be operating more powerfully than those who are engaged in shaping the events may even know. It is remarkable, certainly in the case of American history, the extent to which certain patterns do recur and certain principles are fought over in the same ways. So it may be that the Constitution and certain fundamental principles and contradictions in the American democracy itself are dominating events in a way in which those called upon to shape those events do not fully understand. From that point of view, the very traditional elements in the New Deal do give a consistency to the New Deal, and the mere fact that FDR was an American President in time of crisis meant that he was susceptible to those great traditions. If you were bred in the tradition, as Roosevelt was, these things emerged in time of crisis and ultimately behind them are the theoretical ideas themselves which created this tradition even before Jefferson and Madison and Hamilton fashioned its political foundations.[2]

In other words, Roosevelt was informed by reference to certain political principles, and it is not necessary to argue that he had fully reflected on these principles. They were in the air, and he would naturally come to think about the problems with which he was confronted in terms of *the* political tradition. But, in fact, it seems clear that he did indeed elaborate his intentions; and, with a consideration of political principle in mind, he tried to develop a thoughtful view of what the country ought to do in order to meet the crisis at hand. You cannot speak or act in politics on so grand a scale as Roosevelt did without bringing out in argument some principle or principles of action which can then be further clarified through theoretical analysis.

Roosevelt surely never presented an exact blueprint for a better United States; for, as he believed, what you know theoretically, in advance of the working out of certain reforms, is something different from what you can find out by the experience of those reforms. Therefore it would be imprudent to act on the basis of principle alone in practical political matters. Thus follows his remark: "With such an approach, the New Deal, keeping its feet on the ground, is working out hundreds of current problems from day to day as necessities arise and with whatever materials are at hand. We are doing this without attempting to commit the Nation to any ism or any ideology except democracy, humanity and the civil liberties which form their foundations."[3] Roosevelt is saying that we are not reconstructing a government *on the basis of* any ism or ideology dogmatically asserted, but *in order to achieve* certain specific aims: to stabilize agriculture, to improve the conditions of labor, to safeguard business against unfair competition, to provide the lowest third of the nation with a decent standard of living, to protect our national resources. The worst sort of statesman would be the abstract statesman. The really excellent statesman may be capable of both speculation and action, but he knows which is which and how they are related.

The purpose of this book is to try to understand the character of the Roosevelt Revolution, that is, to try to understand the character of the changes wrought by the New Deal, and the extent to which those changes altered the course of American politics. Our understanding of the American political course will be enhanced by our understanding of the New Deal's contribution to American political thought and practice, for it was at that time that a new way of looking at the relationship between the government and the economy emerged in America. But the transformation of the traditional American democracy into a welfare state, with its regulated or controlled economy, seems more revolutionary than it really is. It is our belief that one of the great lessons of the past thirty years (and this is something Roosevelt clearly understood) is the extent to which America's traditional democratic order has proved compatible with far more welfare and far more regulation than anyone had hitherto thought possible. Roosevelt rejected the paternalistic welfare state when he rejected socialism. So, instead of saying that the traditional American democracy became undermined in the period of the New Deal, it would be more accurate to say that the meaning of American political life underwent a profound reinterpretation at that time. Roosevelt surely redirected the course of American politics very profoundly, for there is no doubt that the welfare state is incompatible with certain features of the traditional American democracy. But Roosevelt, the statesman who introduced the welfare principle, did not consider it a radical change; that is, it was not a change that went to the *root* of the system. It preserves it. The New Deal fulfilled a function that was essentially restorative or conservative rather than constitutive.

In his book *The American Political Tradition*, Richard Hofstadter writes that Roosevelt "stands out among the statesmen of modern American liberalism—and indeed among all statesmen since Hamilton—for his sense of the failure of tradition."[4] Roosevelt surely had no respect for mere tradition. As he told the Daughters of the American Revolution in 1938: "Remember, remember always that all of us, and you and I especially, are descended from immigrants and revolutionists."[5] But Roosevelt's political perspective is that of a man wholly within the American tradition. Moreover, he made it a part of his contribution to the continuity of that tradition to remind the American people of the relationship between their struggle against the depression and the other great struggles in American history. In an address during the 1938 party primaries, he stated: "As in the time of George Washington in 1787, when there was grave danger that the states would never become a Nation—as in the time of Abraham Lincoln, when a tragic division threatened to become lasting—our own time has brought a test of our American Union."[6] It is certain that Roosevelt's correction or reinterpretation of the traditional American democracy which we find in the New Deal is not properly understood if one does not consider the traditional emphasis in his thought.

Franklin Roosevelt stands in the same relation to the American political course as Abraham Lincoln. I doubt that he stands in the same relation to that tradition as James Madison and Alexander Hamilton, for he was a preserver rather than a founder or innovator. If there was one characteristic theme during the New Deal period, it was the preservation or conservation of democratic political institutions. It would be a serious mistake to conceive of the New Deal as partaking merely of reform and change and not as conserving the tradition. Still, the statesman is bound by specific circumstances. Thus, someone who wanted to preserve democracy in 1933 would be confronted by entirely different circumstances or conditions from those confronted by someone who wanted to preserve it in 1860. Roosevelt was aware of this when he said in 1938 that "it seldom helps to wonder how a statesman of one generation would surmount the crisis of another. A statesman deals with concrete difficulties—with things which must be done from day to day. Not often can he frame conscious patterns for the far off future." But he was also aware of the extent to which certain patterns do recur in American history and certain issues are debated in similar ways. Thus, he continued: "... the fullness of the stature of Lincoln's nature and the fundamental conflict which events forced upon his Presidency invite us ever to turn to him for help. For the issue which he restated here at Gettysburg seventy-five years ago will be the continuing issue before this Nation so long as we cling to the purposes for which the Nation was founded—to preserve under the changing conditions of each generation a people's government for the people's good."[7] The mere fact that FDR was an American President having responsibility at a most critical moment in American history means that he was susceptible to the principles and contradictions that make up the tradition in a way in which no other individual at that time was.

The great achievement of Roosevelt's statesmanship consists in his preserving the continuity of the American political tradition. Accordingly, that statesmanship was able to distinguish between rigidly preserving its practices and flexibly preserving its principles. The "Nine Old Men," as the Hughes Court came to be called, saw only preserving rigidly those practices and not flexibly those principles. Within a living tradition, such as the American political tradition, the innovations introduced are not necessarily the opposite of the tradition. They may very well represent its strengthening, and one cannot understand *our* political tradition in its depth unless one understands it in the light of that strengthening. A typical mistake of the conservative is his concealing the fact that the continuous and unchanging tradition he reveres so much would never have come about through conservatism, or without discontinuities, revolution, and upheaval at the very beginning of the tradition. With this thought in mind, Roosevelt pointed out at the beginning of his second presidential campaign that preservation is never simple preservation without any changes. To preserve is to reform. Therefore reform becomes preservation for the farsighted conservative.[8]

Shortly after the court-packing plan was announced in early 1937, Felix Frankfurter wrote to the President that there was no easy way out of the difficulty with the Supreme Court, that all possible courses of action had their advantages and disadvantages, and that any major tampering with the body politic would involve some shock to the body politic.[9] But Roosevelt was willing to take that risk. The Hughes Court had argued that the emergency of the depression did not make a difference. Roosevelt argued that the emergency did make a difference, but he went further than that. He wanted the Court to understand the various currents and trends prevailing in the country, not so much simply to reflect the changing wants and wishes of the populace, but rather to direct them toward the preservation of the principles and institutions of government intended to protect the interests of the society as a whole.

What may help us to understand the New Deal is the fact that periods of crisis have always been periods when the American mind achieved its greatest insights into the nature of politics and political society. The period of the New Deal reveals the innermost character of American politics, for in a crisis what is essentially political is revealed in the extreme. It is a time in which a country takes stock of itself, in which it debates great issues in however confused and vulgar a way. The inevitable consequence, when profound economic and political issues are debated and resolved, is the level of political controversy so characteristic of the New Deal generation.

CHAPTER 3

The Great Depression and the Class Struggle

The Problem of Political Freedom

THE literature on Franklin D. Roosevelt generaly reflects praise from those who call themselves "liberals" and criticism from those who call themselves "conservatives." Both major factions in American politics have been so preoccupied with the intricacies of the class struggle that a proper understanding of Roosevelt's statesmanship has been obscured. The significance of his influence on the course of the American political tradition will be largely missed, we believe, unless we raise our view above the level of the class struggle. The intention of this chapter is to present a view of Roosevelt's statesmanship that moves away from the limits of partisan considerations, whether liberal or conservative. We do not hesitate to assert that such a movement is possible and that it will enable us to see that the actions he took as a statesman were based on a serious and considered understanding of what democracy is, whereas the bulk of the literature, whether praising or blaming him, usually regards his actions as merely "shrewd." Of course Roosevelt was shrewd. But that artificial distinction between shrewdness and idealism overlooks the more important questions of whether he was shrewd for good or ill ends, and whether he was conscious or thoughtful about the relation between shrewd actions and ultimate objectives. In order to answer these questions, we shall need to consider his understanding of the problem of political freedom.

It almost goes without saying that freedom is constantly experienced as a value in our democratic society. Freedom and equality are inseparable expressions of that same thing called democracy, but to the extent that freedom has an appeal which equality has only derivatively, we can still say that freedom is the key word of democracy. As Roosevelt reminded the nation in the final speech of his second presidential campaign: "The American citizen . . . is a product of free institutions. His mind has been sharpened by the exercise of freedom."[1] A free society derives its character by looking up to freedom, but freedom as freedom is always used for something else. Otherwise it would be a formal and empty freedom. It may tentatively be suggested that we live in a society in which everyone is free to pursue happiness as he understands it, and that therefore freedom would be required for the pursuit of happiness. One surely cannot pursue happiness as he understands happiness if he is not free, but this freedom extends only to such pursuit of happiness as is compatible with everyone else's pursuit of happiness. It was John Locke, the first in rank among modern democratic theorists, who wrote: "Freedom is not, as we are told, a Liberty for every man to do what he lists: (For who could be free, when every other Man's Humour might domineer over him?) But a Liberty to dispose, and order, as he lists, his Person, Actions, Possessions, and his whole Property, within the Allowance of those Laws under which he is; and therein not to be subject to the arbitrary Will of another, but freely to follow his own."[2] It would seem, therefore, that whatever it is that constitutes a free society presupposes the pursuit of happiness as the end or goal of freedom, but that that pursuit must be so arranged that a reasonable effort will be made to consider the interests of others along with our own. This is certainly the Lockean premise from which Roosevelt begins.

In a presidential campaign address delivered in 1932, Roosevelt remarked that "we have learned a great deal [about liberty and the pursuit of happiness] in the past century. We know that individual liberty and individual happiness mean nothing unless both are ordered in the sense that one man's meat is not another man's poison."[3] There is, of course, a large and important truth in this assertion that the freedom of the individual is only valid insofar as it does not infringe on the proper freedoms of other individuals. The price of freedom is therefore the restraint of freedom, and the price of freedom for everyone is the restraint on the greater freedoms of some. As Justice Harlan Fiske Stone wrote to Herbert Hoover in 1934: "Today what the Wall Street banker does may have serious consequences on the fortunes of the cotton planter in Mississippi and the farmer in Iowa. The textile manufacturer of New England is at the mercy of the employer of child labor or unpaid labor in the South. He must yield either to the pressure or abandon his business, with all the consequences to his employees and to his community—unless, perchance, the freedom of action of the employer of child labor is to some extent curtailed in the interest of the larger good."[4] Political freedom, as distinct from the freedoms of special persons and classes, is the freedom that can be enjoyed by all members of the political community, and that can exist only insofar as the society is restrained by rules. The restraint on the exploiter becomes the freedom of the exploited, and only through restraint on the actions by which individuals exploit other individuals does the whole political community gain political freedom. In this sense, restraint must be contrasted not with freedom but with only a narrow interpretation of it.

The previous argument suggests that freedom is not necessarily opposed to restraint. Indeed, all political freedom rests on restraint and, as we have indicated, the restraints imposed on one individual or group of individuals become the condition of the freedom of other individuals. As Roosevelt stated in his Commonwealth Club Address in 1932: "Every man has a right to his own property; which means a right to be assured, to the fullest extent attainable, in the safety of his savings. . . . In all thought of property, this right is paramount; all other property rights must yield to it. If, in accord with this principle, we must restrict the operations of the speculator, the manipulator, even the financier, I believe we must accept the restriction as needful, not to hamper individualism, but to protect it."[5] The freedom that has relevance is not the freedom of one individual or group of individuals gained at the expense of others, but the freedom that is dependent upon the completeness with which all members of the political community are restrained from injuring one another. With this thought in mind, the President explained in his Constitution Day Address in 1937 that "the Constitution guarantees liberty, not license masquerading as liberty. Let me put the real question in the simplest terms. The present government of the United States has never taken away and never will take away any liberty from any minority, unless it be a minority which so abuses its liberty as to do positive and definite harm to its neighbors constituting the majority."[6] The assumption here is that freedom presupposes that certain conditions are fulfilled, that is, that the only way in which we can have our freedom is through limitations on freedom.

The American democracy is concerned with freedom, but the only way in which there can be freedom is for there to be such rules and regulations for the conduct of society as will add most to the security (and hence enjoyment) of those freedoms. And among the rules that democratic societies may properly make for their better preservation are those dealing with equality of economic rights and opportunities. In the process of reflecting on freedom, Roosevelt stated that "liberty requires opportunity to make a living—a decent living according to the standard of the time, a living which gives men not only enough to live by, but something to live for. For too many of us the political equality we once won was meaningless in the face of economic inequality. . . . Today we stand committed to the proposition that freedom is no half-and-half affair. If the average citizen is guaranteed equal opportunity in the polling place, he must have equal opportunity in the market place."[7] Therefore political freedom includes, not only freedom of expression, security of person and property, the rights of public meeting and association, but the freedom to organize and bargain collectively, to pursue useful and remunerative employment commensurate with one's ability, and so on. And a regime that fosters these things is a good regime.

We have been led, as was expected, to the awareness that individuals are free to direct their own activities only insofar as other individuals are prevented from injuring and exploiting them. So far there is no significant departure from the fundamental tenets of individualism. But Roosevelt went further. He clearly saw our democratic system's tendency toward oligarchy in the absence of a regulation of capitalism. He was concerned with the effects of the unequal distribution of wealth on the society as a whole. Moreover, he connected economic inequality with the threat to freedom, which necessitated, as he believed, modifying and controlling private economic enterprise. Accordingly, the New Deal imposed controls on the investment process, forced reductions on the size of public-utility holding companies, and the like. Indeed, private enterprise had become too private, for private enterprise had lost its sense of directedness toward the public interest. Certainly the founders of the doctrine of private enterprise had never allowed themselves to become entranced by the mechanics of the market and matters of mere self-interest. Only a small boy could be entranced by the former and only a small man by the latter considerations.

Roosevelt made completely clear the break with the earlier liberalism, which break had been anticipated by the measures of Theodore Roosevelt and Woodrow Wilson. Even if fairly considerable modifications of the earlier liberalism, already made by TR and Wilson, had prepared the way for the later break, nevertheless a sense of the fundamental defect in Jeffersonianism was necessary for that break. To indicate the departure from Jeffersonianism which Roosevelt's thinking represents, we must realize that he would never have said, as Jefferson did, that constitutions should have no longer tenure than the approximate life of one generation. Nor would he assume, as Jefferson did, that the powers of the national government were restricted by the Constitution to those enumerated plus those absolutely necessary to carry those that were enumerated into effect. In his address to the Young Democratic Clubs in 1935, he shows the consequences of extreme individualism without showing the collapse of that individualism:

> The cruel suffering of the recent depression has taught us unforgettable lessons. We have been compelled by stark necessity to unlearn the too comfortable superstition that the American soil was mystically blessed with every kind of immunity to grave economic maladjustments, and that the American spirit of individualism—all alone and unhelped by the cooperative efforts of Government—could withstand and repel every form of economic disarrangement or crisis. . . . [But] let me emphasize that serious as have been the errors of unrestrained individualism, I do not believe in abandoning the system of individual enterprise. The freedom and opportunity that have characterized American development in the past can be maintained if we recognize the fact that the individual system of our day calls for the collaboration of all of us to provide, at the least, security for all of us. Those words "freedom" and "opportunity" do not mean a license to climb upwards by pushing other people down.[8]

But once Roosevelt takes the consequences of Jeffersonian individualism into account, he ceases to be Jeffersonian. As he had stated in his Commonwealth Club Address: "Where Jefferson feared the encroachment of political power on the lives of individuals, Wilson knew that the new power was financial. He saw, in the highly centralized economic system, the despot of the twentieth century, on whom great masses of individuals relied for their safety and their livelihood, and whose irresponsibility and greed (if they were not controlled) would reduce them to starvation and penury."[9] In considering the problem of individualism, in other words, Roosevelt makes explicit what was already implicit in his thinking about the earlier liberalism.

The President was deeply concerned about the danger to our freedoms caused by economic inequality, and as a result of that concern there evolved in his mind an understanding of the problem of freedom which went beyond the Jeffersonian understanding. The problem of freedom, as Roosevelt suggested, is necessarily concerned with economic as well as with political considerations. In other words, freedom must be construed as consisting not only in security of political rights, but also in guarantees that the economically weak will not be at the mercy of the economically strong. In the circumstances of a highly centralized industrial system, Roosevelt believed, the defined and limited freedom which alone can be generally enjoyed is most likely to be secured by a regime that restrains inequalities as well as one that concerns itself with the virtues of individual enterprise, and this constitutes a marked departure from the earlier liberalism.

But we are compelled to move a step further; for, without recourse to a deeper principle than that which we have thus far had, we seem unable to transcend the individualism of the earlier liberalism. We have already seen that political freedom rests on restraint, and that the broadening of that freedom may necessitate increased restraints on the particular freedoms of some individuals. But when such restraints are denounced as infringements on freedom, we are forced to ask: for what purpose are the restraints intended? The restraints derive their justification from the kind of action they curtail, or in the kind of society in which such restraints (and freedoms, for that matter) are exercised. In this sense, it is no longer a matter of increasing and decreasing restraints, but of organizing them to secure conditions believed necessary for the common good. Therefore the clue to a deeper understanding of freedom is suggested by our recourse to the notion of the common good, and concern for freedoms and restraints is overshadowed as concern for the common good or justice comes into view.

Roosevelt's view of the common good or conception of justice adds up to a preference for the greatest good of the greatest number.[10] If we take what he regarded as the good political scheme, the end or purpose of government is the greatest good of the greatest number. The greatest good of the greatest number may very well appear to be the good of everyone, but it is actually the good of the large majority, perhaps even the good of the common people as distinguished from the good of the wealthy. The greatest good of the greatest number may even require severe limitations on the freedom of the wealthy to some extent. The problem of freedom therefore becomes one of finding that point of coincidence between freedom and restraint on which the greatest good of the greatest number, or the political common good, rests. For Roosevelt, justice is the political common good and justice is a kind of equality. Everyone, Roosevelt believed, should have a truly equal opportunity in the pursuit of happiness. In defining the problem of the relation of freedom to justice, Roosevelt stated: "The thing we are all seeking is justice—justice in the common-sense interpretation of that word—the interpretation that means justice against exploitation on the part of those who do not care much for the lives, the happiness and the prosperity of their neighbors."[11] We have seen that the political common good requires a balancing and harmonizing of freedoms and restraints. Roosevelt's New Deal did not wish to place property at the mercy of the propertyless or freedom at the mercy of the propertied. The New Deal attempted to achieve the right mean, not by avoiding restraints on the processes of the economy on the one hand and the freedoms of the individual on the other, but by integrating restraints and freedoms into a regime that could provide for the greatest good of the greatest number.

In the course of this argument, we have been carried beyond the horizon of freedom. Freedom implies restraint, but the purposes for which governments choose to exercise those restraints is the crucial political consideration. Those choices determine to a large extent the character of the society in which we live. Roosevelt wrote to David Sarnoff in 1940 that "in order to maintain our American system of private initiative and private enterprise, it must function as a system that will do the greatest good for the greatest number. It is only by keeping our economy socially conscious that we can keep it free."[12] It was precisely at this point that the President was confronted with these paramount political questions: Is the American democracy a good or just democracy? And in recognition of its deficiencies (which were obviously there) how can the American democracy improve itself? Indeed, Roosevelt's quest for a broader understanding of freedom, a freedom that includes equality of economic rights as well as equality of political rights, has carried us to deeper questions (of which the President himself was perhaps only dimly aware) relating to the aims and justifications of a democratic political society. The Great Depression seems to have proved that serious-minded men cannot abandon the question of the good or just society. At any rate, we have learned that the problem of freedom is inseparable from the problem of justice, since freedom is the freedom to act in ways that are either just or unjust or somewhere in between. Mere freedom may produce majority tyranny, and, in order to have democratic relevance, freedom must ultimately be understood in terms of what is just. Political freedom therefore is a means to justice or the just ordering of society, and not an end in itself.

The basic thing to be remembered is that every freedom, which is freedom for something, necessarily limits freedoms and therefore establishes a distinction between freedom and license. It makes freedom dependent on the end for which it is intended. There can be no question that a democratic society requires dedication to freedom, but this dedication does not come merely from the enjoyment of freedom. It requires something more. It requires a humane concern for the happiness and well-being of all the members of society. We are not trying to examine the whole problem of democratic values here, but are merely trying to suggest what would be involved in the restoration of that understanding of freedom joined with social justice or the common good. Roosevelt moved in that direction.

Democracy and the Class Struggle

The great issue of the twentieth century, the issue between liberal democracy and Marxian communism, is whether or not man must be collectivized in order to be free. According to the Marxists, only as a member of a society that is not subject to its own products, meaning a society that owns (as well as controls) the means of production, can an individual be free. That societal ownership will be effected in the proper way, according to Marxian doctrine, only as a culmination of the class struggle which has raged increasingly from earliest times to the present epoch but which, also according to that doctrine, can and will be culminated or transcended through the materialist dialectic of history. If we are properly to grasp Roosevelt's statesmanship, we must grasp his view of the class struggle and its relation to liberal democracy. Is it inevitable? Is it permanent or is it, on the contrary, a historical thing and therefore something which cannot be transcended? If it can, but will not necessarily, be transcended, are we better off with it or without it? If it is to remain, either necessarily or by choice, how ought liberal democracy to deal with it? Whether the actions Roosevelt took as a statesman contributed substantially to the proper or just ordering of our democratic institutions, and whether those actions are based on a serious and considered understanding of what democracy is, depends upon the answers to these questions.

The President told the 1937 annual meeting of the National Housing Conference that "we have come to realize that a Nation cannot function as a healthy democracy with part of its citizens living under good conditions and part forced to live under circumstances inimical to the general welfare."[13] A democracy ceases to be a democracy when the regime is directed toward the benefit of a small part and not toward the benefit of the large majority. When Roosevelt tried that same year to secure wages and hours legislation, he cautioned the Congress that "a self-supporting and self-respecting democracy can plead no justification for the existence of child labor, no economic reason for chiseling workers' wages or stretching workers' hours."[14] But once it is admitted that there are possibilities for improving an existing society, the question concerning the character of the good society becomes paramount. For we really cannot understand the Social Security Act, the National Labor Relations Act, the Fair Labor Standards Act, and other crucial pieces of New Deal legislation unless we consider them in terms of their intention to secure a better quality of life for the members of our democratic society. These reforms point toward an understanding of the essential character of the good society, or at least of the liberal democratic understanding of the good society.

In his treatise on the English Constitution, Walter Bagehot observes that

the leading statesmen in a free country have a great momentary power. They settle the conversation of mankind. It is they who, by a great speech or two, determine what shall be said and what shall be written for a long time after. . . . [The] ordinary mind is quite unfit to fix for itself what political question it shall attend to; it is as much as it can do to judge decently of the questions which drift down to it, and are brought before it; it almost never settles its topics. And in settling what these questions shall be, statesmen have . . . a great responsibility. If they raise questions which will excite the lower orders of mankind; . . . if they raise questions on which the interests of those orders is not identical with, or is antagonistic to, the whole interest of the state, they will have done it the greatest harm they can do.[15]

Raymond Moley argues that Roosevelt deliberately overstated the issues involved in the economic crisis of the 1930's by talking about the great industrial and financial interests as money-changers and economic royalists, and hence gave too exaggerated an encouragement to the proletarianization of American life. FDR leveled the charge of "money-changers" against the big interests in his first inaugural address and complained of "economic royalists" in his second presidential campaign, giving the impression of a conspiracy on their part.[16] Moley states that "Roosevelt has never condemned businessmen . . . as a whole. He always qualified his denunciations with references to the 'small, bad' minority in these groups. But the fact that he has limited himself to denunciations of the 'small, bad' minority in these specific groups and ignored the 'small, bad' minority in all other groups has been just as effective in developing class antagonism as a general denunciation. An administration that leaves more rather than less consciousness of class has done the country a disservice."[17] The issue cannot be avoided by asserting that Roosevelt denied any hostility on his own part to the interests of industrialists or bankers. He knew how to disarm his adversaries by making them appear to be enemies of the people, which, in a sense, they were.

To what degree does class self-consciousness make class struggle? What are the facts regarding the quantum of class-consciousness in the United States in the 1930's? What did

Roosevelt do about it? What did he say about what he was doing and what did he say in order to get it done? Surely Roosevelt's statesmanship cannot be seen apart from the class struggle, because statesmanship involves dealing with concrete circumstances and the circumstances here involved the class struggle more than anything else. A very large part of the country was disaffected by massive dislocations in the economy, and he used the rhetoric of the class struggle in order to persuade the *demos* that his was a sympathetic ear. Indeed, the rhetoric of the class struggle was one of the facts of political life that had to be accepted or approved or stolen in order to be moderated. That is, appreciable moderation might very well involve riding the crest of the rhetoric of that which was being moderated. And under the circumstances of the Great Depression, moreover, Roosevelt had every right, and even an obligation, to start from the premise that the common good was equivalent to the immediate interests of the many as many, and, more precisely, to the economic interests of the many. His battle against the "economic royalists," or in plainer language, the rich, took the form of a limitation on their freedoms, a limitation he conceived to be in the common interest or for the common good. But essentially what we shall try to show is that the notion of the common good implicit in his statesmanship was of a higher order than that implicit in the Marxian doctrine of the class struggle, for he rejected the radical egalitarianism of that doctrine.

Writing of Roosevelt and the New Deal in 1934, Winston Churchill wondered

> whether the rigid and comparatively moderate structure of American trade unionism [would] be capable of bearing the immense responsibilities for national well-being and for the production of necessities of all kinds for the people of the United States which the power now given to them implies. . . . Our trade unions have grown to manhood and power amid an enormous network of counter-checks and consequent corrections; and to raise American trade unionism from its previous condition to industrial sovereignty by a few sweeping decrees may easily confront both the trade unions and the United States with problems which for the time being will be at once paralysing and insoluble.[18]

These doubts were written prior to the passage of the NLRA of 1935, which represents the culmination of labor's entire effort. Churchill may have been thinking specifically about section 7a of the National Industrial Recovery Act of 1933, or perhaps about Public Resolution No. 44, which created the NLRB in 1934, and the spurt to union activity accomplished by these provisions. Or conceivably he was thinking of the ill-fated Wagner Labor Disputes Act of 1934. But the fact is that Roosevelt's extreme cautiousness pervades the whole controversy over the recognition of collective bargaining during the early New Deal period. Churchill's doubts were unwarranted in 1934. As subsequent events showed, these same comments could not properly have been made later on.

There was nothing radical about section 7a. It simply affirmed the right of employees to organize and bargain collectively through representatives of their own choosing and, conversely, the obligation of employers not to interfere with that right by forcing their employees to join company-dominated unions. Actually, the right to organize and bargain collectively had been conceded before the New Deal, although the effectiveness of that right was always dependent upon the willingness of employers to recognize their organizations and bargain with them. The right of employees to organize and bargain collectively is meaningless without a corresponding obligation upon the employer to bargain with representatives once elected. And the protection of free organizing and bargaining in this statute turned on the obligation of employers not to compel their employees to join company unions. But this statute did not outlaw company unions. And even if the majority of the workers designated an independent trade union as their bargaining agent, employers were still free to bargain only with the minority who designated no representatives at all or a company union. If anything approximating equality of bargaining power is to be achieved, the employer must bargain exclusively with an independent trade union chosen by a majority of the workers representing *all* the workers.

So the presence of section 7a on the statute books placed employers under no specific obligation to recognize and bargain with self-organized and independently represented employees. And the employers were still free to form company-dominated unions when it suited their convenience. As a result, representation disputes occurred which ended in industrial strife. Therefore 7a needed amendment to meet these new circumstances. Accordingly, the President issued a February 1, 1934, executive order authorizing the National Labor Board (there was not yet a National Labor Relations Board) to conduct representation elections under the majority rule principle. But two days later Hugh S. Johnson of the National Recovery Administration and his general counsel, Donald R. Richberg, issued a statement interpreting that order to mean that minority groups and individuals still had a right to bargain separately with their employers. The Labor Board preferred the presidential order on its face and ruled in the Denver Tramway case on March 1 that representatives elected by a majority of the workers were the exclusive bargaining agents. It is against a background of these conflicting interpretations of the meaning of section 7a and the refusal of a large number of companies even to recognize the Labor Board's authority that Senator Robert F. Wagner of New York introduced the labor disputes bill into Congress on March 1.

The essential provisions of the labor disputes bill of 1934 were the authorizing of a new labor board to hold representative elections and require management to bargain with the designated representatives of a majority of the workers, and the imposing of severe limitations on company union activities. In a Senate hearing on the bill, Franklin S. Edmonds, the general counsel for the Philadelphia Chamber of Commerce, declared that it impressed him as having been written by "a man who had been reading Marx on Class War, and thought that all employees and employers were standing in opposite corners making faces at each other."[19] But disagreements between labor and management arise out of the concrete conditions of modern industrial life and, to the extent that collective bargaining removes vast inequalities in income distribution, it has had a moderating rather than an aggravating effect on the class struggle. As the Supreme Court later indicated in the Jones and Laughlin Steel case: "Experience has abundantly demonstrated that the recognition of the rights of employees to self-organization and to have representatives of their own choosing for the purpose of collective bargaining is often an essential condition of industrial peace. Refusal to confer and negotiate has been one of the most prolific causes of strife. This is such an outstanding fact in the history of labor disturbances that it is a proper subject of judicial notice and requires no citation of instances."[20]

Still the President was unwilling to support the labor disputes bill. But after months of mounting labor unrest and the imminence of a threatened nationwide steel strike, he proposed Public Resolution No. 44 on June 12 as a substitute for that bill. This resolution provided for the creation of a National Labor Relations Board with authority to hold elections to determine which group represented a majority of the employees and to compel the employer to recognize them for collective bargaining purposes. Senator Wagner came out in support of the resolution, stating that it might be a good thing "to allow the reforms of the past year to encounter an additional year of trial and error, so that the processes of education and understanding may catch up with the social program that has been inaugurated." He continued: "That is the judgment of the President with regard to the labor-disputes bill, and I am prepared to go along with him. No one is in a better position to weigh the program in its entirety."[21] The newly created National Labor Relations Board, authorized under this resolution, reaffirmed the majority rule principle in the Houde Engineering and Auto Workers case. But that principle was not established in statute law until the passage of the National Labor Relations Act of 1935. In its essentials, that act was modeled on the labor disputes bill of the previous year. It affirmed the majority-rule principle and outlawed the company union. Although the President did not take part in developing it, he did come out in its support after it passed the Senate. And just three days after his announcement, the Supreme Court invalidated the NRA, including the collective bargaining provisions of section 7a and Public Resolution No. 44 which amended it. The Court had nothing to say about the constitutionality of 7a, but the entire machinery of collective bargaining collapsed nevertheless. Therefore the passage of the new labor relations bill became imperative, and Roosevelt helped to push it through the House of Representatives.

The rather prominent position of the National Labor Relations Act within the New Deal as a whole sometimes gives the impression of a radical Roosevelt. But his labor policy emerged gradually. The President's stopgap improvisation, Public Resolution No. 44, was introduced in response to a threatened nationwide steel strike, but that resolution provided for the first National Labor Relations Board whose interpretation of section 7a eventually became incorporated into the National Labor Relations Act. And that act was the result of a search for workable and equitable procedures for determining wages, hours, and other conditions of employment. The President's endorsement came after fifteen months of consideration and only after voluntary compliance had been given every conceivable opportunity to work. Interestingly enough, after the Court had invalidated the NRA, Vice-President Garner advocated a constitutional amendment to enlarge the powers of Congress over the nation's industries. It is always instructive, when the chips are down, to see Roosevelt's more "conservative" critics like the Vice-President and Raymond Moley proposing measures that would alter existing democratic institutions far more radically than anything the President would ever have suggested.

Just eight years after the British General Strike of 1926, the trade union movement's antagonist in that strike, Winston Churchill, stated: "The trade unions have been a stable force in the industrial development of Britain in the last fifty years. They have brought steadily to the front the point of view of the toiler and the urgent requirements of his home, and have made these vital matters imprint themselves upon the laws and customs of our country. They have been a steadying force which has counterbalanced and corrected the reckless extravagances of the Red intelligentsia."[22] As it was conceived under the New Deal, collective bargaining was predicated on an understanding that was the very antithesis of the class-struggle doctrine. The Madisonian analysis in *Federalist* ten must be appreciated here: the problem is how the struggle between classes in the Marxist sense can be avoided in a large commercial republic like the United States. Madison's solution to that problem turns on achieving the right kind of divisiveness. In the course of his analysis, he enumerates two kinds of divisions coming from property: differences according to the amount of property men possess and differences according to the kind of property they possess. The differences over the amount of property were the basis for the traditional class struggles in the ancient regimes. And the possibility for subordinating differences over the amount of property to differences over the kind of property stands or falls upon the immediate limited advantages that workingmen can secure in their specialized trades or their callings within a trade. In other words, the society as a whole will be fragmented into many narrow limited interests rather than into classes. The struggle between interests will replace the struggle between classes. But for the Madisonian scheme to work, as it has worked, there must be no unusual obstacles that prevent men from pursuing their limited and immediate interests, and their gains must be real, that is, a reasonably high level of wages and satisfactory working conditions. Otherwise the scheme would soon cease to mollify the fragmented interests, and the latent struggle between the classes as classes would burst forth.[23]

But what does the Madisonian diversity of interests have to do with collective bargaining, where the whole tension is between the employees in one firm and the management of that firm (industry negotiation makes no difference here)? Certainly the tension between labor and management is not the same as the tension between, say, all the people (employees and owners alike) in the banking business on the one side and all the people in farming, or in retail trade, or in transportation, or in manufacturing on the other. The experience of American history graphically illustrates that trade unionism, through the procedure of collective bargaining, has tended to lessen the sharpness of the class struggle and thereby permit the Madisonian diversity of interests to flourish more readily. And taking the sting out of the class struggle tempers the public's tendency to focus its attention on the class struggle, thus improving things all around. As the President stated in his first Fireside Chat of 1936:

> In other countries the relationship of employer and employee has been more or less accepted as a class relationship not readily to be broken through. In this country we insist, as an essential of the American way of life, that the employer-employee relationship should be one of free men and equals. We refuse to regard those who work with hand or brain as different from or inferior to those who live from their property. But our workers with hand and brain deserve more than respect for their labor. They deserve practical protection in the opportunity to use their labor at a return adequate to support them at a decent and constantly rising standard of living, and to accumulate a margin of security against the inevitable vicissitudes of life. The average man must have that . . . opportunity if we are to avoid the growth of a class-conscious society in this country."[24]

Inasmuch as class consciousness is a contributor to the class struggle second only to the existence of a massive underprivileged class, a democratic regime is made inherently more stable by virtue of the moderation of the interests of its classes. In constantly seeking to strengthen labor, Roosevelt recognized and exercised that moderation.

Roosevelt had a humane man's dislike of poverty, probably a belief that poverty makes men worse in a certain way, and a democrat's prejudice against inequality. It was his understanding that the wastes and destructions resultant from radical economic inequalities require that a sufficient provision be made for a more equitable distribution of the nation's wealth. Collective bargaining contributes to such a redistribution. In his 1935 annual message to the Congress, the President explained that in removing economic inequalities "we do not seek to destroy ambition, nor do we seek to divide our wealth on stated occasions. We continue to recognize the greater ability of some to earn more than others. But we do assert that the ambition of the individual to obtain for him and his proper security, a reasonable leisure, and a decent living throughout his life, is an ambition to be preferred to the appetite for great wealth and great power."[25] Roosevelt's thought is this: a good democratic society is essentially defined by the completeness of the common good it pursues. And the common good itself demands a reasonable security and a pleasant living within the limits of the possible for the whole political community. A democracy based on radical economic inequalities, which can only result in irreconcilable opposition between the propertied and the propertyless, becomes ever less democratic until it ceases altogether to be liberal democracy, and becomes, instead, the mob rule of ancient democracy, or oppressive tyranny by the greedy few.

On the occasion of the Supreme Court's invalidation of the NRA, an editorial in the *New Republic* stated: "Either the nation must put up with the confusions and miseries of an essentially unregulated capitalism, or it must prepare to supercede capitalism with socialism. There is no longer a feasible middle course."[26] As a matter of fact, the entire New Deal program was predicated on the assumption that such a middle course *was* possible. It involved a considerable interference with private property. It operated on the assumption that government is entitled to interfere with property and, to some extent, to foster the redistribution of property. Roosevelt was in favor of private property, but he was not opposed to government interference with property, which he conceived to be in the public interest or for the common good. Inheritance taxes and corporation taxes tend to interfere with the property right in itself, without actually destroying property. In other words, the emphasis was on private property, but not necessarily on private property wholly at the disposal of the individual or the individual corporation. FDR argued, moreover, that laws could be passed limiting the accumulation of property, or rules could be established for the use of property, or vigorous governmental action could be taken to redistribute property or to benefit the propertyless, and that we could still have a free economy.

Roosevelt understood that an essentially unregulated capitalism leads to concentrated private power, the nakedness and violence of the class struggle, and ultimately to socialism. As he stated to the Congress in 1938: "Capital is essential; reasonable earnings on capital are essential; but misuse of the powers of capital or selfish suspension of the employment of capital must be ended, or the capitalistic system will destroy itself through its own abuses."[27] And this is precisely why Marxism teaches that capitalism, simply speaking, leads inevitably to socialism by its own logic. What we have evolved in America is a semifree or controlled capitalism, that is, an economic system which the government *regulates*, but does not *operate*. But the radical advocates of free private enterprise have never seemed to understand that government regulation is not socialism. And that if properly guided, it prevents socialism. Roosevelt was dealing with unexampled economic circumstances that had brought clearly into question the basic Madisonian assumption that modern liberal democracy could arrest and even overcome the wastes and destructions of the class struggle. Precisely because he regarded the class struggle as *permanently* inevitable (rather than historically inevitable as Marx does) he hoped to *moderate* it rather than, as Marx hoped, to *exacerbate* it so that it can, dialectically, be transcended.

Raymond Moley's charge is that Roosevelt did the wrong thing in the depression. But the charge behind Moley's charge is that to do *anything* is the wrong thing. For the government to leave old laws and modes of economic relations standing—and to refuse to introduce new laws and new modes—in the midst of radical changes in the material conditions is *itself* governmental redistribution of property, for the old modes were set by government in the light of *old* conditions. Not to change the modes in harmony with the changing conditions is just as much governmental activity as is the harmonious changing of modes. And the changing of modes is in some ways more preservative of the status quo, for not to change denies one segment of society its proportionate share and hence redistributes the proportions. But our point here is simply this—that there is no such thing as government "leaving the economy alone," for the economy does not stand still—it moves.

What Walter Bagehot teaches us about the power of those who set public conversation has perhaps greater force in a criticism of Moley than in a criticism of Roosevelt, for Moley and other conservative critics of the New Deal have helped promote the false notion that public concern for distributive justice is the preserve of Marxism. This would seem to imply that whenever a difficult problem presents itself, the best solution would be the avoidance of any solution, or to let time take care of the problem. The difficulty with this proposition was revealed in the near collapse of our liberal democratic regime in the Great Depression.

CHAPTER 4

Roosevelt: Conservator of the American Political Tradition

ALL political life concerns itself with preservation or change, that is, with the very practical business of deciding what to preserve and what not to preserve. Hence it is always salutary to be provided with critical comments on our traditions and practices, for criticism surely points in the direction of remedies. But, more important, criticism forces us to think seriously about what we hold worthwhile as a nation, or to reevaluate our traditions. Richard Hofstadter presents his book *The American Political Tradition* as a "reinterpretation of our political traditions," and as a guide for the future.[1] As he indicates, especially at a time when "the traditional ground is shifting under our feet," it is imperative to gain "fresh perspectives" on our traditions.[2] And this means gaining fresh perspectives on the men, or the careers of the men, who made those traditions. Hofstadter himself has a sense of the failure of the tradition. He sees the liberal tradition as "rudderless and demoralized." What is needed is a "new conception of the world" to replace "the ideology of self-help, free enterprise, competition, and beneficent cupidity."[3] Certainly Hofstadter is right in suggesting that a properly ordered democracy requires something more than beneficent cupidity or covetousness. But we seriously wonder whether his reduction of the tradition, or rather the public leaders who made that tradition, to their lowest common denominator points in the direction of the democratic realism he seeks.

The particular leaders whom Hofstadter selects for his "studies in the ideology of American statesmanship" were chosen because they best represented or reflected the tradition.[4] Presumably, therefore, he understood the tradition before he made his selection. His final essay entitled "Franklin D.

Roosevelt: The Patrician as Opportunist" contains a discussion of a remarkably representative leader. Roosevelt achieves particular relevance as a statesman, in Hofstadter's understanding, by virtue of his being sensitively attuned to the play of political forces around him. He is characterized as a "warmhearted, informal patrician" who believed that "if a large number of people wanted something very badly, it is important that they be given some measure of satisfaction."[5] And we are told that "although the influence of great men is usually exaggerated, Roosevelt must be granted at least a marginal influence on the course of history. No personality has ever expressed the American popular temper so articulately or with such exclusiveness.... [He had] a sharp intuitive knowledge of popular feeling. Because he was content in large measure to follow public opinion, he was able to give it that necessary additional impulse of leadership which can translate desires into policies."[6] In other words, Roosevelt not only helped to influence but especially reflected the American popular temper.

To measure Roosevelt as a statesman means to measure how he *influenced* as well as how he *reflected* the American popular temper. And if there were parts of our popular temper that he really influenced or fashioned, he could not at the same time have reflected them. But Hofstadter does not preserve this distinction. Therefore, what was in the popular temper or mind and what was in the mind of Roosevelt becomes blurred. In his introductory essay, Hofstadter explains that his study aims to analyze "men of action in their capacity as leaders of popular thought, which is not their most impressive function." It is less important, he continues, "to estimate how great our public men have been than to analyze their historical roles."[7] But unless we examine what makes our leaders great or influential, how will we be able to learn what happened to their aims and principles in the course of American history? In other words, how would we know what their historical roles really were?

Hofstadter has conceded that "the New Deal marked many deviations in the American course" and that Roosevelt must be granted at least a marginal influence on the course of American history.[8] But what is the character of these marginal influences and deviations? The New Deal, says Hofstadter, had left "upon the statute books great measures of permanent value." And we may reasonably assume that he has in mind such measures as the Social Security Act, the National Labor Relations Act, and the Fair Labor Standards Act, all of which are mentioned in his Roosevelt essay. Hofstadter further states that the New Deal established "the principle that the entire community through the agency of the federal government has some responsiblity for mass welfare, and it has impressed its values so deeply on the national mind that the Republicans were compelled to endorse its major accomplishments in election platforms."[9] Here, as Hofstadter himself admits, Roosevelt had put something into, or impressed something upon, the national mind, and in this sense his statesmanship constituted something more than a mere expression or reflection of the national mind.

Hofstadter's emphasis on the representative rather than the innovative character of our public leaders reveals itself in his first essay, entitled "The Founding Fathers: An Age of Realism." Consider, for example, his remark that "despite their keen sense of history, [the Founding Fathers] felt they were founding novel institutions and glorified in the newness of what they were doing."[10] Apparently the Founding Fathers were not founding novel institutions at all. According to Hofstadter, what they wanted was known as "balanced government," an idea "at least as old as Aristotle and Polybius," and this "ancient conception" had received "new sanction in the eighteenth century."[11] This notion of balanced government, Hofstadter continues, was most clearly elaborated by John Adams, who believed that "the aristocracy and the democracy must be made to neutralize each other" and that "each element should be given its own house of the legislature."[12] Presumably the point of view of the Founding Fathers which Adams was reflecting was that the Senate was meant to be *aristocratic* and the House of Representatives *democratic*, and that these aristocratic and democratic elements would neutralize each other. But was the Senate really intended to be an aristocratic institution? And did the Founding Fathers really mean to secure a mixed or balanced republic, that is, to secure a balance between aristocratic and democratic elements within the confines of a republic?

Hofstadter would be correct in suggesting that the Founding Fathers conceived of the Senate as a safeguard for property rights. But *safeguarding* property rights is not the same thing as *representing* property rights. As Madison understood the distinction: "The senate there [meaning the House of Lords], instead of being elected for a term of six years, and of being unconfined to particular families or fortunes, is an hereditary family of opulent nobles."[13] But membership in the American Senate required no property qualification, and senators were to be appointed or elected in a manner prescribed by the state legislatures which, in turn, were elected by the people. Hence the Senate, as it was actually proposed in the Constitution, was intended to operate only in a way (and these are Madison's own words) that would be consistent with "the genuine principles of republican government."[14] It was not intended as an aristocratic body.

Obviously the English Parliament provided the Founding Fathers with the model of a divided legislature. But the intention of a divided legislature in the English Parliament was to secure a balance between aristocratic and democratic elements. And this was connected with the pre-modern preference of Aristotle and Polybius for a mixed or balanced government. For Aristotle and Polybius, the mixture of forms within the framework of a single government contributed to its stability. The defects of the simple forms would be cancelled out, and hence it would last longer than any of the simple forms. But the parceling out of different kinds of powers to different branches and sub-branches of government, installed by the Founding Fathers, had a decidedly different emphasis than the arrangements contemplated by Aristotle and Polybius and operative in the English Constitution. The Founding Fathers had no notion whatsoever of introducing an aristocratic element into their system through the mechanism of divided legislative power. Their concern was far more with the liberty of the individual than with the security of the state, or at least they tended to see the maintenance of republican institutions as a means of safeguarding individual liberties. Separation of powers was intended to prevent the concert of representatives in any scheme of oppression against the liberties of the people. Hofstadter's failure to separate the intent of the mixed government of the English Constitution from that of separation of powers in the American Constitution could only result in the depreciation of the innovations of the Founding Fathers. He does concede that the debates over the Constitution were carried on "at an intellectual level that is rare in politics, and that the Constitution itself is one of the world's masterpieces of practical statecraft."[15] But as a whole the innovations of the Founding Fathers are greatly deemphasized, as is the innovative statesmanship of Roosevelt.

The main thrust of Hofstadter's criticism of Roosevelt and the New Deal is that the President failed to think through the organic ills of society and therefore to achieve a more realistic conception of what was happening in the world.[16] For example, Roosevelt saw the development of big business and monopoly as a threat to democratic institutions, but he was "equivocal" about how the threat was to be controlled. Hofstadter continues: "Although [Roosevelt's] argument carried to the brink of socialism, it was not socialism he was proposing. . . . How the reformist state was to police the corporations without either destroying free enterprise or itself succumbing to the massed strength of corporate opposition was not made clear. Roosevelt did not tackle such problems in theory, and events spared him the necessity of facing them in practice."[17] But the alternatives, as Roosevelt well understood, need not be socialism or the corporate state. In recommending the regulation of public utility holding companies to Congress in 1935, the President explained: "I am against private socialism of concentrated private power as thoroughly as I am against governmental socialism. The one is equally as dangerous as the other; and the destruction of private socialism is utterly essential to avoid governmental socialism."[18] Perhaps Hofstadter is somewhat impatient with the moderate Rooseveltian answer to the problem of big business and monopoly, namely, government regulation. And government regulation, if properly guided, prevents the destruction of private enterprise. Roosevelt made precisely this assumption. We must recognize that Roosevelt was a statesman and that he was trying to get certain things done. Therefore, he had to make some very practical decisions, as, for example, whether at a given time a particular enterprise should or should not be regulated or whether there should be more or less regulation in certain industries. But in order to measure his performance as a statesman, as Hofstadter suggests, we would need to consider whether he thought very deeply about what he was trying to get done as well as the practical wisdom of his actions.

What about the President's proposal to reform the Supreme Court in 1937? Was he able to place that proposal in some broader political perspective? Or was he simply caught up in the immediate issues of that controversy? In a later book, entitled *The Age of Reform*, Hofstadter argues that Roosevelt's fight with the Supreme Court was begun "not in the interest of some large democratic principle," but because the Court's decisions made it impossible for him to achieve "a managerial reorganization of society." Roosevelt's first concern was not that judicial review was "undemocratic," but that the federal government had been stripped of its power to deal effectively with economic problems. If he had opened up the whole question of the propriety of judicial review in a democratic society, Hofstadter continues, he would have been following a more "high-minded approach." But instead Roosevelt offered the pretense that the advanced age of the justices prevented them from performing their judicial duties. And it remained for Senator Burton K. Wheeler, whom Hofstadter describes as a "principled man," to propose an amendment to the Constitution permitting Congress to override judicial vetoes of its own acts.[19] Roosevelt's approach was presumably *unprincipled*, that is, unrelated to some large democratic principle.

Soon after the court-packing plan was announced, Arthur Krock of the *New York Times* interviewed the President, and the latter made it clear in that interview that the issue was in his estimation "but part of a larger problem." As Krock relates the President's views: the President sees a future "far more dangerous if he is balked of his solutions than if they are adopted. He sees a growing belief among the underprivileged that judicial supremacy is certain to cancel the progressive and humanitarian efforts of Congress and the Executive. He sees this belief easily firing into desperate conviction; and he does not happen to doubt, should this happen, a leader will arise to tread down democracy in the name of reform." And Krock continues: "The President has not forgotten Huey P. Long. While he does not say so in precise words, he entertains the opinion that one important reason why the Louisiana Dictator was not able to extend his dominion further during his lifetime was because he was fortunately coexistent with wiser and more sincere remedies for the conditions which produced Long." And had public opinion against the Hoover administration "not been sufficiently formed by the election of 1932, and had Mr. Hoover therefore been re-elected, the President believes that Huey Long would immediately have become a menace to the democratic process."[20] But Hofstadter understands the President's opposition to Long primarily in terms of his threat to the Democratic ticket in 1936. A secret poll had been taken in 1935, and the Democratic National Committee was concerned about the Louisiana governor's strength. And Hofstadter relates that Raymond Moley was "horrified" to hear Roosevelt speak about the need for doing something "to steal Long's thunder."[21] But what Hostadter has not considered is the fact that Roosevelt, even before he became President, referred to Long as "one of the two most dangerous men in the United States" and at that time indicated the need for doing something about him.[22]

We must not forget that Franklin Roosevelt and Adolph Hitler came to power within a few months of each other. Hitler actually became German chancellor in January, 1933. And Roosevelt never overlooked the possibility of a similar occurrence in the United States. One of the original members of the Brains Trust, Rexford G. Tugwell, relates a conversation in 1932 which reveals Roosevelt's uneasiness: "There was latent, he thought, not far below the uneasy surface of our disrupted society, an impulse among a good many . . . men used to having their own way, mostly industrialists who directed affairs without being questioned, a feeling that democracy had run its course and that the totalitarians had grasped the necessities of the time. People wanted strong leadership; they were sick of uncertainty, anxious for security, and willing to trade liberty for it."[23] In his 1940 Annual Message to Congress, the President stated "that dictatorship—and the philosophy of force that justifies and accompanies dictatorship—have originated in almost every case in the necessity for drastic action to improve internal conditions in places where democratic action for one reason or another has failed to respond to modern needs and modern demands."[24] Roosevelt continually emphasized the lesson of history "that dictatorships do not grow out of strong and successful governments, but out of weak and helpless ones."[25] As the experience of the present time, not to mention that of the recent past, serves to show, in Southeast Asia and elsewhere, the dictatorship of the proletariat is considered preferable to the status quo if the status quo means disease and starvation. And in such circumstances any change is regarded as a change for the better. One of the President's favorite quotations was: "The most dreadful failure of which any form of government can be guilty is simply to lose touch with reality, because out of this failure all imaginable forms of evil grow."[26] It was his considered opinion that the Supreme Court majority in its opposition to crucial New Deal reforms had simply lost touch with the economic realities of the period.

Hofstadter seems to take it for granted that the principle of judicial review, which the President did not seek to circumscribe, is "undemocratic." But as the Founding Fathers well understood (not to mention Woodrow Wilson and Franklin Roosevelt), a democratic regime requires certain checks or controls on the mechanism of majority rule in order to maintain itself because every regime has within itself the seeds of its own destruction. The practice of judicial review is very much a part of our democratic tradition; and it was recognized as such by the President despite his charges, during the course of the court fight, that the Supreme Court had been misconstruing the Constitution. Surely, challenging the Court's interpretation of the Constitution is not the same thing as restricting the right of the Court to interpret the Constitution. The President was not willing to do the latter. He properly characterized Senator Wheeler's proposed amendment that Congress be permitted to override judicial vetoes of its own acts as "an attack upon the very function of the Court and upon the legitimate exercise of that function." And he went on to say that he was not prepared, nor did he consider it advisable, to undermine "one of the foundations of our democracy."[27] In a letter to Joseph M. Patterson, written before the court-packing plan was ever presented, the President expressed the hope that "the problem created for the nation by the Supreme Court" could be faced and solved "without getting away from our underlying principles."[28] And "without getting away from our underlying principles" required, as far as the President was concerned, the retention of the principle of judicial review.

Certainly, as Hofstadter states, the President's first concern was that "the federal government had been stripped . . . of its power to deal with economic problems." But surely the preservation of a democratic regime, or the ability of a democratic regime to deal with its own crises, economic or political, is in line with "large democratic principles" which give to that regime its "democratic" character. Prior to the announcement of the court-packing plan, the President stated that "we have come to realize that a nation cannot function as a healthy democracy with part of its citizens living under good conditions and part forced to live under circumstances inimical to the general welfare."[29] The democratic society which then existed was essentially a good society, but in the President's estimation many improvements still needed to be made. And if these improvements were not made, there existed the possibility of that society's degenerating to the point of collapse, and fascism emerging in its wake. The President believed that there was a real danger to the nation if the Supreme Court majority persisted in its attempt to invalidate crucial New Deal measures. Indeed, his struggle with that Court was begun in the interest of some large democratic principle, and that was the perpetuation of our democratic institutions. And he chose to accomplish this objective without altering the traditional power of the Supreme Court, which in fact would have amounted to a change in the Constitution in the broader sense. But why shouldn't Roosevelt have been concerned with the future composition of the Supreme Court? No matter how highly one regards the institution, that institution cannot generate its own wisdom—it is the wise men on the Court who make wise decisions. And wise justices are appointed by wise Presidents. Therefore he *was* able to see the court-packing plan in its broader political perspective and realize its central significance in the politics of the New Deal period.

Hofstadter states that his studies have convinced him that more emphasis needs to be placed on the "common climate" of American opinions within our political traditions. But, as he observes, the existence of this climate has been obscured by "the tendency [of historians] to place political conflict in the foreground of history." The conflicts are constantly reactivated, while the commonly shared convictions are most of the time neglected.[30] But how can the study of history and especially political history properly be separated from political conflict? Is not political conflict, or the struggle between competing groups within the political community, the very crux of political history? And how can Roosevelt be understood apart from political conflict when it is in political conflict or crisis that he achieved his greatest insights into the nature of politics and political society? We must read Roosevelt, as well as our other influential political leaders, not primarily as representatives of the public mind, but for what we can learn about how they *influenced* the course of our national life. But in order to make such an estimate, we must examine, in the case of Roosevelt, the important political conflicts or crises of his career; for it is in political crisis, acting under the pressure of events, that the President was drawn to "the depths of the problem," and it is here that his deepest thoughts are revealed.

Hofstadter characterizes Roosevelt as "a public instrument of the most delicate receptivity" and thus arrives at the conclusion that his successes as a statesman were based almost wholly upon his responsiveness to what the people wanted, and his ability to translate those wants into public policies. He was a more flexible and cleverer politician than Wilson but "less serious, less deliberate, and less responsible."[31] But as Roosevelt's handling of the crisis of the Great Depression showed, he understood very well what it means to be *responsible for* as well as *responsive to* the public interest or need. He once suggested that most of the great accomplishments in American history had been made by Presidents who so "truly" interpreted the "needs" and "wishes" of the people that they were supported in their great tasks by the people.[32] But of course "needs" are not the same as "wishes" and are sometimes opposed to wishes. What the people wish for may fall far short of their needs, and may in fact be detrimental to or even destructive of their needs or necessities. If the people as a whole were always able to determine what their needs really are, there would be little conflict between needs and wishes. And sometimes, as in a crisis, needs are more easily discernible or more visible than at other times. As Roosevelt reflected: "It is only in a crisis that we look back to our common concerns. The stress of a vast emergency rudely awakes us all from our local concerns and turns us to wider [or public] concerns."[33] But at other times the needs will appear less obvious and hence there will be a conflict between needs and wishes. To interpret the needs and wishes of the people, as Roosevelt suggested, would require pointing the wishes of the people in the direction of their needs. Indeed, to convince the people to wish for what they really need is the Herculean task of the democratic statesman. This task is made Herculean because a democratic people is the ultimate judge as to what constitutes its needs. What Roosevelt attempted was to point the American democracy in the direction of its needs within the most difficult context of democracy.

The epigraph at the beginning of Hofstadter's introductory essay reads as follows: "In times of change and danger when there is a quicksand of fear under men's reasoning, a sense of continuity with generations gone before can stretch like a lifeline across the scary present."[34] But this quotation does not really reflect his understanding of our present situation, for our sense of continuity with generations gone before, as he sees it, would be a very *inadequate* lifeline indeed. This quotation comes from a chapter in John Dos Passos' book *The Ground We Stand On* entitled "The Use of the Past." But Hofstadter's epigraph contains only part of the sentence. The last part, which is omitted, reads: "... and get us past that idiot delusion of the exceptional." As it appears in Dos Passos, the full sentence reads: "In times of change and danger when there is a quicksand of fear under men's reasoning, a sense of continuity with generations gone before can stretch like a lifeline across the scary present and get us past that idiot delusion of the exceptional."[35] In other words, a sense of tradition has salutary effects, not the least important of which is ridding ourselves of that "idiot delusion" that our times are "exceptional" times. And Dos Passos states also: "... our problem is not so very different now [from that of the Founding Fathers]."[36] As the full statement suggests, Dos Passos is recommending the recovery of a tradition, not for the sake of transcending it, but for the sake of *using* it. And, as he advises, if we fail to cope with the problem of adjusting the industrial machine to human needs, "it won't be for the lack of a political tradition."[37] That is, he believes we already have a satisfactory political tradition from which to work, and our failing is the neglect of that tradition. Hofstadter believes that Roosevelt's shortcoming was his failure to transcend the American political tradition. But our view is that Roosevelt thought clearly and well on that tradition. Not so much because tradition itself is unambiguously good; but because ours is a good tradition, and because he believed it to be not only good but also sufficiently open to the progressive solution of the current problems without radical change. Roosevelt *chose* not to transcend the tradition. His was a deliberate, a deliberated, conservatism.

As we have previously indicated, the whole burden of Hofstadter's thesis, the introductory essay notwithstanding, is that

Americans need a new conception of the world or a clearly articulated break with the traditional or inherited faith, and *not* a sense of continuity with generations gone before.[38] But Dos Passos says that the "world picture" the Founders had was one of "the grandest and most nearly realized world pictures in all history."[39] And therefore, "in times like ours, when old institutions are caving in and being replaced by new institutions not necessarily in accord with men's preconceived hopes, political thought has to look backwards as well as forwards."[40] Certainly, Dos Passos continues, we would need to know "which realities of our life yesterday and our life today we can believe in and work for," but the permanent basis for the world picture into which we can fit our present lives is afforded by the traditions and habits of the Founding Fathers.[41] Hofstadter says that Americans have found it more convenient to see where they have been than where they are going.[42] But Dos Passos says that we need to know what kind of "firm ground" other men, belonging to generations before us, have found "to stand on."[43] Hofstadter actually reverses the Dos Passos thesis, for he recommends a *break* with the tradition. But we never learn what the character of that break should be like or in what direction that break should move. It would then appear that Hofstadter's impatience with Roosevelt is based upon Roosevelt's failure to found wholly new modes and orders. *Our* question is whether Roosevelt's or Hofstadter's understanding of the importance of continuity is the better.

CHAPTER 5

Roosevelt versus the Hughes Court

The Use and Abuse of the Constitution

BY 1933, the Great Depression had produced an economic crisis unparalleled in American history, and the National Industrial Recovery Act of that year was part of a comprehensive effort made by the New Deal Administration to remedy the depressed state of the nation's economy. The Recovery Act grappled with that depression as it directly affected labor and industry, and there was a reliance placed upon the commerce power as sufficient in itself to support the Act. But a unanimous Supreme Court's invalidation of the NRA in May, 1935, in *Schechter Poultry Corporation* v. *U.S.* brought the whole structure of New Deal regulatory legislation into jeopardy. The NRA was declared unconstitutional ostensibly because it delegated legislative power to the President, but a more specific act of Congress could have remedied that. Far more crucial was the Court's determination that the trade and labor practices of the Schechter Poultry Corporation might not be regulated by the national government under its power over commerce among the several states. The importance of this determination issued from the fact that it threatened all economic regulatory legislation based on the commerce clause of the Constitution. Therefore, the real question behind the Court's decision that Congress could not delegate legislative power to the President was whether Congress ever had the legislative power under the commerce clause to regulate the business of the Schechters in the first place.

The crucial political issue of the 1930's was the extent of the economic regulatory powers of the national government allowable under the commerce clause. The problems of the depression were economic, and the commerce clause was the constitutional power most directly concerned with economic matters. Hence, the legislation directed at controlling or regulating many aspects of the national economic system was principally predicated upon that clause. In his famous "horse and buggy" press conference, the President discussed the Court's narrow construction of the commerce clause as the most significant aspect of the Schechter decision.[1] He wanted a more comprehensive meaning to be attributed to the commerce clause, and he wanted the constitutional enumeration of the fundamental powers of government to be interpreted with enough flexibility to accommodate the new regulatory activities of the national government. It is most important here to observe how Roosevelt, in taking up the question of the extent of the commerce clause, enlarged and refined our understanding of the American Constitution.

Foremost among the criticisms of President Roosevelt and the New Deal was the charge that their understanding of the Constitution had departed significantly from the essentially democratic character of the American political tradition and had moved in the direction of centralization. And those Supreme Court justices whose great concern was caused by the centralizing tendencies of that administration contended that a comprehensive commerce power would obliterate the distinction between what is local and what is national and result in a decisively centralized nation. Justices Willis Van Devanter, James McReynolds, and George Sutherland obviously wanted to block the New Deal, and they saw the Constitution as an instrument that deprived the country of any power to enact national economic legislation. They saw it as such because of the supposed necessity of maintaining the states in their powers over their local concerns. After the Schechter decision, even Justice Brandeis, who had little in common with the Van Devanter-McReynolds-Sutherland group, told one of the President's closest advisors, Tom Corcoran: "This is the end of this business of centralization, and I want you to go back and tell the President that we're not going to centralize everything. It's come to an end. As for your young men, you call them together and tell them to get out of Washington—tell them to go back to the states. That is where they must do their work."[2] Brandeis further believed, and has been quoted as saying, that "the United States is too big to be a force for good; whatever we do is bound to be harmful. . . . The United States should go back to the federation idea, letting each state evolve a policy and develop itself."[3]

Whatever one might think of Brandeis's extreme attack on New Deal policies, the important thing about it is that it constitutes a restatement of the old-fashioned argument that the smaller unit should have a greater significance in American politics. As he had written to Paul U. Kellogg in 1920:

> The great America for which we long is unattainable unless that individuality of communities becomes far more widely developed and becomes a common American phenomenon. For a century our growth has come through national expansion and the increase of the functions of the Federal Government. The growth of the future . . . must be in quality and spiritual value. And that can come only through the concentrated, intensified striving of smaller groups. The field for special effort shall be the State, the city, and the village—and each should be led to seek to excel in something peculiar to it. If ideals are developed locally—the national ones will come pretty near to taking care of themselves.[4]

Brandeis wanted a political system that would be as free as possible from centralized direction, and hence would not sap the vitality of the local communities. Bigness, as he saw it, was a curse. The argument for federalism (or what we may more properly call decentralist federalism) is that it prevents centralization and therefore mitigates some of the evil effects of bigness. Centralization, moreover, is seen as having something to do with a loss of freedom.

For our present purposes, we will limit ourselves to a discussion of the commerce clause aspect of the Schechter decision, which was the most important part of that decision, although, as we have indicated, the invalidation of the NRA rested on the supposed unconstitutionality of the delegation of legislative power. As regards the commerce clause, the government lawyers argued that the trade and labor provisions of the NRA were part of "a comprehensive effort [made] by Congress to remedy the breakdown in interstate commerce which culminated in 1933. In this view, practices which contribute to sharp decline in wages, prices, and employment, contribute to a frustration of commerce among the States and are subject to federal regulation in the interest of protecting and promoting that commerce."[5] What the government lawyers tried to show was that intrastate wages and the like have an effect on the price of the product or the purchasing power of the employees and ultimately on interstate commerce. On this point the Court answered through its Chief Justice that the national government may not regulate the wages and hours of local businesses as part of a nationwide plan for restoring and distributing purchasing power, no matter how great the public need. If it could deal with wages and hours "because of their relation to cost and prices and their indirect effect upon interstate commerce," then "all the processes of production and distribution that enter into cost could likewise be controlled."[6] How long the Schechter employees should work and how much they should be paid was too remote or "indirect" in its effect on interstate commerce, and it did not even matter that there was a serious economic crisis in the country.

It is important for us to see that the Court is claiming that only intrastate activities "directly" affecting interstate commerce could be regulated by the national government under the commerce clause; no matter how consequential, an "indirect" effect would not be enough. For the national government to be able to regulate activities not themselves interstate, such activities must directly affect interstate commerce. This opinion is based on the assumption that there is "a necessary and well-established distinction between direct and indirect effects," which "must be recognized as a fundamental one, essential to the maintenance of our constitutional system."[7] If the national government had the power to regulate everything that had an indirect effect upon interstate commerce, the Court argued, "there would be virtually no limit to the federal power and for all practical purposes we should have a completely *centralized* government."[8] Therefore the trade and labor practices of businesses that process and sell for local consumption must be seen as having only an "indirect" effect, or otherwise the states might not be able fully to exercise their reserved powers over their local concerns, which the perpetuation of the federal system requires. In other words, the distinction between direct and indirect effects on interstate commerce constitutes a guarantee that the distinction between what is national and what is local will not be obliterated and thereby create a completely centralized government.[9] As a matter of fact, the American Constitution makes no mention of direct and indirect effects on interstate commerce, but it does authorize Congress to make all laws which can be justified as implied from or a necessary means to its enumerated powers, which includes the commerce power.

The Court's understanding of the Constitution, as stated by

Chief Justice Charles Evans Hughes in the Schechter case, was that increased activities by the national government, penetrating deep into the local communities, violates the traditional federal division of local and national functions, and that that violation prepares the way for dangerous centralization. The decisive premise of this whole argument is that there is a province of freedom with which the national government is not entitled to meddle. One way of controlling the national government and hence guaranteeing that freedom is to maintain a system in which, according to that understanding, the powers of government are distributed among various levels of government. However important economic stability is, it was freedom that finally assumed an overriding importance in the Hughes Court's treatment of New Deal regulatory legislation, at least prior to the court-packing plan, and freedom was held to depend on a federal division of powers. It is hardly unreasonable to suppose that the Hughes Court was radically democratic and reactionary at the same time, for it seemed to think that the Constitution means whatever freedom means, and freedom, as the Court understood it, is emphatically an aspect of modern democracy. But the fact that the Constitution which delineates the American system of government is in general democratic and is, in its entirety, aimed at the preservation of democratic freedom does not mean that every aspect of that Constitution unrelievedly favors particular elements of freedom.

The Schechter case was, in our opinion, a "landmark" case for three reasons: first, it was a unanimous decision written by the Chief Justice rather than by a member of the conservative faction (with a concurring opinion of Cardozo's indicating no departure from the commerce clause aspect of that decision); second, it was substantially a commerce clause decision (although the legislation in question was not invalidated on these grounds) in that the crucial argument concerning the threat to the federal system turned on the doctrine of direct-indirect effects; and third (and following from the second), the unanimity of that opinion was understood at the time to constitute a threat to all future New Deal regulatory legislation based on the commerce clause.

The critical question, as Roosevelt saw it, was whether or not the national government could be entrusted under the Constitution with the task of dealing with national economic problems and economic crises. He had to defend a very large increase in the regulatory powers of the national government as being constitutional and his understanding of the Constitution gave the national government the necessary power (unless specifically prohibited in particular clauses of the Constitution) to alleviate national economic emergencies. There was no reason to suppose that the national government was intended to be confined to mere delegations of power, especially in the light of the necessary and proper clause. But Roosevelt knew that the problem of determining the extent of the national commerce power, important as it was, was not the fundamental problem. A power is a *means* by which certain *ends* are accomplished. The powers delegated to the government or to certain branches of the government are powers to do certain things or perform certain tasks and are therefore related to certain ends or purposes of government. Those ends after which the particular powers of government are drawn as means are specified in the Preamble to the Constitution. Roosevelt conceived of a national government as having powers fully adequate to accomplish the ends or purposes that the Preamble sets forth, but not transcending those ends. In a Fireside Chat concerning his controversy with the Court, Roosevelt argued for the extension of national power, while preserving the essential purposes of the government as stated in the Preamble. "In its Preamble, the Constitution states that it was intended to form a more perfect Union and promote the general welfare: and the *powers* given to the Congress to carry out those *purposes* can be best described by saying that they were all the powers needed to meet each and every problem which then had a national character and which could not be met by merely local action."[10] The inference here is that you have to relate the particular powers stated in the Constitution to the purposes of government stated in the Preamble, and not abstract the commerce clause from the whole body of the Constitution. The Hughes Court, however, misread the broad language of the commerce clause in the Schechter case and, reviewing the argumentation of that Court's opinion, we are moved to conclude that FDR had a better understanding of the scheme of the Constitution. The commerce clause permits a flexibility that the Hughes Court simply refused to recognize.

One of the greatest difficulties with the American Constitution is that it *seems* to decide once and for all which objects are to be dealt with nationally and which are to be dealt with locally. But surely the distinction between what is national and what is local is not that unalterable, for the activities treated as local when in isolation could, under the circumstances of a nationwide economic crisis, become of vital national concern. What the Hughes Court failed to appreciate was that the decision whether to do a thing nationally or locally (in this case the proper extent of government control over the economy) must always be a prudential decision made at the particular moment in view of the particular circumstances. That Court, moreover, did not pay sufficient attention to the harsh economic circumstances of the depression or to the fact of the pervasive interdependence among all the different processes in the nation's economic life.

Indeed, it can be argued that the intrastate and interstate aspects of the nation's economy are inseparable because there is scarcely any intrastate activity in a highly integrated economic system like our own that does not affect or is not affected by interstate commerce. Therefore, one can reasonably conclude that the power of the national government extends, through the commerce clause, to the regulation of the economy as a whole in order to provide for the general welfare or the common good. The Great Depression demonstrated certain inescapable realities. Surely one of these realities was that the general welfare or common good requires a *limitation* on freedom, a limitation that can be imposed only by government. The Hughes Court tried to make the Constitution an instrument to deprive the United States of economic legislation in the interest of preserving freedom. This effort allows us to say that the Hughes Court's misunderstanding of freedom caused it to lose sight of some of the great objects of government, such as that of providing for the general welfare. It is probably not an overstatement to assert that its overriding concern with freedom (that is, that the economy should be allowed to act on its own without substantial government regulation or control) was the crucial failing of the Hughes Court.

It has always been thought, since the most obvious action of Roosevelt's New Deal was the reform of democratic institutions, that he was an innovator. But he did not actually institute any reform that resulted in a major change in the American Constitution. From the rash of Supreme Court decisions in 1935–1936 invalidating crucial New Deal measures to the court-packing crisis in 1937, Roosevelt was absorbed with the danger to the American Constitution which he saw in the Court's view rather than with any desire on his own part to change it. He wanted to make certain that the Constitution remained in harmony with the fundamental requirements of the nature of the regime. His understanding of that danger emphasized the Hughes Court's strained or narrow construction of the commerce clause.[11] That Court handed down a series of decisions, the cumulative effect of which amounted to a corruption of the Constitution, for a majority of that Court attempted to sever the practical connection between the commerce power and the needs of the country which the commerce power was originally intended to serve. The question of the relationship between the polity and the economy therefore was obviously central to that great political confrontation between the Hughes Court and the President.

The Hughes Court was faced with New Deal statutes of a most controversial character, representing as they did a marked departure from the traditional conceptions of the partition of power between the states and the nation, and accordingly many members of that Court resisted the trend of these statutes. One can go further and say the Supreme Court went askew in 1935 because the moment had occurred for a prudential change in practice that the previous constitutional tradition had frowned upon. It is instructive at this point to remind ourselves that there may be times when the Court, within its proper limits, may resist a certain trend in legislation, and there may be other times when judicial self-restraint is the order of the day. The Court needs to know when legislation should "go fast" and when it should "go slow." But this knowledge requires a full understanding of what fast and slow really mean in all cases, crisis or not; and that understanding, in the case of the New Deal statutes in question, would necessitate a realistic appraisal of the economic conditions prevailing in the country. The Hughes Court's error was not its refusal, prior to the reelection of President Roosevelt in 1936, to budge in the face of popular demand. Popular demand was not that unified (especially with regard to such statutes as the NRA). And, of course, it is possible to have popular demand go in the wrong direction. The Constitution, moreover, ought not to mean whatever popular opinion wants it to mean, at a given moment. The Hughes Court's error was its refusal to face up to the hard and unpleasant problems of the Great Depression, given the economic realities of the times, *and* the simple falsity of its representation of the constitutional document.

The crucial controversy of the New Deal period prior to 1937 was whether the Constitution prohibited the national government from dealing with the problems of a nationwide integrated economy (outside the field of public utilities) no matter how great the public need. Even as late as April, 1937, in the Labor Board cases, four justices were arguing that the principles of the Schechter and Carter cases still applied, and that therefore the regulation of relations between employees engaged in manufacturing was an unconstitutional exercise of the commerce power.[12] The big question for the Hughes Court during that period was deciding which things, under the various clauses of the Constitution, should be done by which level of government. That Court challenged the NRA, which was avowedly based on the commerce clause, with the argument that the enterprise of the Schechters was too remote from interstate commerce. It argued that the national commerce power had to cease before it touched the Schechters because, if the trade and labor practices of businesses that process and sell for local consumption were removed from state power, the states would lose some of the autonomy reserved to them by the Constitution. Any effort to increase the regulatory activities of the national government to the point of its participation in purely local functions would mean increased governmental centralization. So the argument of the Hughes Court was that increased governmental centralization would be the inevitable outcome of more national regulatory legislation.

The constitutional revolution of 1937 was represented by the expansion of the limits of the commerce power so as to make the power to regulate commerce the power to regulate the national economy. The prime duty of the Supreme Court is to interpret the law. Therefore it is supposed to say what the law is. But that duty to say what the law is is not always simple. It may very well lead to some far-reaching interpretations. For example, the Court can enlarge the meaning of the commerce clause, through the necessary and proper clause, and thereby enlarge the powers of the national government, although one could hardly make the meaning of the commerce clause any larger than John Marshall made it in *Gibbons* v.

Ogden in 1824. The Hughes Court believed that a commerce power intended to exercise the function of economic regulation would introduce a radical and impermissible change in the system. That Court seemed to assume that democracy requires that the regulatory activities of the national government be suppressed in the interest of freedom, and it carried its inquiry no further than that.

The Court-Packing Crisis

The struggle between Roosevelt and the Hughes Court in 1937 was one of the most serious struggles between two coordinate branches of the government in American history. It was no tempest in a teapot. It represented a severe breakdown in cooperation between two great branches of government. The Court's action, in striking down major New Deal legislation, threatened the virtual shutdown of the entire New Deal program. The Schechter Poultry, Railroad Retirement, and Carter Coal cases reflected the attitude of the Hughes Court toward the exercise of national authority under the commerce power prior to 1937. That Court believed that the legislation under consideration in these cases would push centralization too far. As Cardozo had stated in the Schechter case: "There is a view of causation that would obliterate the distinction between what is national and what is local in the activities of commerce.... Activities local in their immediacy do not become interstate and national because of distant repercussions.... To find immediacy or directness here is to find it everywhere. If centripetal forces are to be isolated to the exclusion of the forces that oppose and counteract them, there will be an end to our federal system."[13] The maintenance of federalism was considered necessary for achieving a necessary decentralization which, in turn, would guarantee freedom; that is, freedom was held to depend on the proper division of governing functions. That proper division between national and state authority, moreover, was understood to be spelled out in the Constitution.

Roosevelt regarded the New Deal program by the end of 1935 as "fairly completely undermined."[14] The view of the commerce clause expressed by the Court in the Schechter Poultry, Railroad Retirement, and Carter Coal cases had largely emptied that clause of any substantial power. It seemed foolish for Roosevelt to propose new legislation while the Court assumed its present posture. Moreover, court injunctions had paralyzed the enforcement of the National Labor Relations Act and encouraged great corporations to defy it. Nearly every important New Deal act rested under a legal cloud. Old-age benefits and assistance, unemployment compensations, the Securities and Exchange Act, the relief acts, the Public Utility Holding Company Act, and many taxing acts were involved in litigation, and there was no definite assurance of what their fate would be. In looking forward to the practical consequences of the Hughes Court's decisions, the major question in the President's mind at the end of 1936 was what the national government might do in the future (say, in the second New Deal administration) with respect to the regulation or control of the nation's economy. As Rexford G. Tugwell remarked, "The Judges had gone too far."[15] Accordingly, Roosevelt sent his proposal to reform the judiciary to the Congress in early February, 1937.

The President's proposal recommended that, when any judge of any federal court had served ten years and had not resigned within six months after reaching the age of seventy, a coadjutor might be appointed to the same bench. It also recommended that the numbers of any bench should be increased by coadjutors, but that the Supreme Court should not have more than six additional members. The proposal focused on the inefficiency of the Court, on injustices caused by delays, and on the inability of the aged justices to understand present-day issues.

The charge was made that this would give the President the virtual power of a dictator and make the Supreme Court subservient to one man. But the President's proposal was not so radical. It merely recommended changing the size of the Supreme Court, which had been often done in the past. It had started in 1789 with five members. This would have enabled the President, by a very slight change of judicial personnel, to secure constitutional decisions favorable to national reform legislation. Such a change was bound to come about anyhow, within a short while. But he could not know *how* short a while, and he had good reason to wonder whether or not the country could wait. Roosevelt was unalterably opposed to making any change in the Constitution, or in the powers of the courts. The device he settled upon was the least radical of all possible ways of reforming the Court, for it altered neither the constitutional powers of the Court nor the extent of its jurisdiction.

The court-packing proposal was an attempt to change the balance of power between those justices on the Supreme Court who took a narrow view of the constitutional powers of Congress and those who took a broad view. Although he would rather not have had to lock horns with the Court and its wily Chief Justice, Roosevelt foresaw no intense hostility to his plan in the Congress. He did not anticipate that the opposition to his proposal would become a rallying point for conservative Democrats opposed to the thrust of New Deal regulatory legislation. Roosevelt went ahead with his proposal for the following reasons: first, so many important New Deal laws had been declared unconstitutional, a large number by five-to-four and six-to-three decisions; second, the Court decisions of 1935–1936 threatened the completion of the New Deal in the second Roosevelt administration; and third, the New Deal had a resounding victory in the 1936 elections, which suggested to the President that he had the full support of a majority of Americans (including the Democrats in the Congress) in any move against the Court. But in spite of his powerful hold on the American electorate, Roosevelt was unable to convince a Congress overwhelmingly controlled by his own party to agree to an enlargement of the Court.

Those actions, precipitated by the opposition, which contributed to the defeat of the court-packing bill were: Chief Justice Hughes's letter to the Senate Judiciary Committee arguing that the Supreme Court was perfectly capable of handling its business and that an increase in the number of justices would not increase the efficiency of that Court; the sudden about-face of the Court's position on the constitutionality of minimum wage and collective bargaining legislation;[16] and the announcement by Justice Van Devanter that he would retire at the end of that Court's present term, thus giving FDR his first appointment to the Court. But the Court's reversal of its previous position on the constitutionality of critical New Deal laws, which contributed to the court-packing bill's defeat, was the very thing that bill sought to accomplish in the first place. Therefore, once a reversal in the course of the Court's decisions had occurred, there was no longer any real need for passing the court-packing bill. Roosevelt was undoubtedly angered by the failure of its passage, but that was a small price to pay, given the Court's reversal of its previous position.

It could be argued that the indirect way in which Roosevelt attacked the Court in 1937, avoiding such questions as how supreme the Supreme Court ought to be and precisely what obedience to it requires, contributed to the defeat of the court-packing proposal. But that argument fails to account for the fact that conservative Democrats (from whom the brunt of the opposition to the proposal came) were looking for a way to oppose the President without making it obvious that they were opposed to the great New Deal reforms. In that sense, opposition to the proposal became the rallying point for conservative Democrats and helped to crystallize their opposition to the New Deal. Although the court-packing fight seemed to worsen Roosevelt's relations with the conservative Democrats, that deterioration in relations was virtually inevitable given the character of the Roosevelt Revolution. His break with the conservative Democrats would have come sooner or later.

The New Deal sought to interpret the commerce power broadly to justify regulation of all the interrelated elements of the national economy, while the Hughes Court sought to interpret that power more narrowly. Roosevelt disagreed with interpretations of the Constitution rendered by a majority of the justices on the Hughes Court. He therefore sought to alter the personnel of that Court so as to alter the balance between liberal and conservative justices and thereby secure another interpretation of the Constitution. He preferred to tamper with the personnel on the Court rather than to tamper with the Constitution. Robert M. Jackson clearly reflected Roosevelt's views when he stated, before the Senate Judiciary Committee hearing on the court-packing bill, that

> our constitutional history abundantly demonstrates that it is impossible to foresee or predict the interpretation or effect which may be given to any language used in an amendment. . . . It may be possible by more words to clarify words, but it is not possible to change a state of mind hostile to the exertion of governmental powers. To offset the effect of the judicial attitude in recent decisions it would be necessary to amend not only the commerce clause and the due-process clause, but the equal-protection clause, the privileges and immunities clause, the tenth amendment, the bankruptcy power, and the taxing and spending power.[17]

Chief Justice Hughes is portrayed by his biographer as being caught in the squeeze between conservative justices who sought to petrify the law and liberal politicians who were determined to ride roughshod over the Court if necessary to reach their goals.[18] Hughes's own objectives are articulated as keeping sensitive to the vibrant realities of his own day and at the same time preserving the constitutional system.[19] But Franklin Roosevelt had no intention of allowing anyone to ride roughshod over the Supreme Court of the United States. Hence, Hughes's middle ground was no middle ground at all; at best it was vacillation. He presided over a Court that attempted to keep the national government out of the economic marketplace in a period of severe economic crisis.

Roosevelt's court-packing proposal was no attack on the Supreme Court as an institution or on its power of judicial review. His deliberate refusal to try to amend the Constitution shows us that. His quarrel was with the decisions of that Court (and hence with the men who made those decisions) at a particular moment in history, and what he proposed was perfectly compatible with, if not exactly similar to, what other Presidents had done in the past. Hughes was incorrect in stating that the passage of the court-packing bill would have destroyed the Supreme Court as an institution. Roosevelt's willingness at a later time to override the two-term tradition was far more radical than his court-packing proposal, radical in the sense that it departed from a well-established tradition. Roosevelt's court-packing proposal was as fully constitutional as he had argued (for the Constitution says a good deal about the jurisdiction of the courts, but nothing about their organization) and, given the apparent state of affairs in February of 1937, a perfectly sensible plan of reform.

CHAPTER 6

The Roosevelt Purge: The Principled Basis of Political Party

THE principle of the American political tradition is that liberalism is the right way of political life, and that moderate democracy is the best vehicle of that liberalism. What liberalism means received profound emphasis and redefinition during the period of the New Deal, for Roosevelt was one of the most important modern elaborators of that term. We can study the 1938 purge of Democratic congressmen with a view to understanding his elaboration of American liberalism. In the course of that struggle, Roosevelt made clear what he meant by liberalism through his distinction between liberal and conservative congressmen in the Democratic party. What we will consider in this chapter is the way in which his attempt to drive "conservative" Democrats out of the party provided the opportunity for identifying that party with the principles embodied in the New Deal.

The President was unwilling to play the party game according to the traditional rules. He initiated and openly supported the American Labor party in New York City as a way of attracting the kinds of votes he believed the Democratic party was incapable of attracting; and he often found it easier to work with Progressive Republicans and Independents than with the Democratic party organization. FDR was going to purge the party because it had nonbelievers in it, and he supported another party which was likely to have lots of believers in it; that is to say, the Democratic party represented *too many* points of view to suit him.

The President's relations with his own party were never more strained than they were in 1938. His attempt to "purge" that party of some of its dissident elements revealed an intraparty controversy of monumental proportions, for the most articulate criticisms of New Deal policies and programs came from within the confines of the Democratic party itself rather than from the opposition party. FDR's influence over certain elements within the party was already deteriorating in 1937 after the court-packing plan was presented to the Congress. That plan unleashed a storm of congressional criticism, but it only accelerated a reaction that was already in the making, for there were plenty of anti–New Deal Democrats waiting for an opportunity to attack Roosevelt without making it appear that they were opposed to his policies and programs. The Democratic party was beginning to slip out of their hands and, even more, it was beginning to look like a different party.

The hard core of that opposition to Roosevelt was constituted by a group of primarily Southern senators, which included Millard Tydings of Maryland, Edward Burke of Nebraska, Walter F. George of Georgia, Ellison D. ("Cotton Ed") Smith of South Carolina, Peter G. Gerry of Rhode Island, Josiah Bailey of North Carolina, and Carter Glass and Harry F. Byrd of Virginia, who voted quite consistently against New Deal "welfare" and regulatory legislation. Some indication of their opposition can be seen in their voting records on four major bills up for passage in the 1937–1938 period—the court reform bill (voted to be sent back to committee on July 22, 1937); the Black-Connery wages and hours bill (first voted on July 31, 1937);[1] the Wagner-Steagell low-cost housing and slum clearance bill; and the government reorganization bill. All eight of these senators voted against the first of these bills (that is, to send it back to committee), and each of the other three bills was opposed by some six of the eight. George, Glass, Byrd, and Bailey voted against all four bills; Tydings, Smith, and Burke voted against three out of four; and Gerry voted against two out of four (not voting at all in the case of the Wagner housing bill).

These senators, moreover, had been active as New Deal opposition prior to the appearance of the court reform bill (in 1935 and 1936), as is indicated by their final votes on the Wagner-Connery labor relations bill, the public utility holding company control bill, the wealth-tax bill, the Social Security bill, the Guffey-Snyder bituminous coal conservation bill, and the Wagner-Ellender housing bill. All eight senators voted against the coal conservation bill, seven against the public utility control bill, five against the wealth-tax bill, four against the labor relations bill, and two against the housing and Social Security bills. Byrd and Burke voted against five out of six bills; Gerry, Smith, and Tydings against four (Smith not voting on one bill and Tydings not voting on two); and George, Bailey, and Glass against three (although Glass would have voted against two others if he had been present).

When the President decided to move against the "opposition" Democrats in the 1938 party primaries, administration candidates were selected to oppose Senators Smith, Tydings, and George, and Representative John J. O'Connor of New York, Chairman of the House Rules Committee.[2] He chose to influence those primaries by means of a charge that certain elements in the Democratic party, who claimed that they were progressive-minded, nevertheless proceeded to stand in the way of all measures intended to carry out liberal objectives. Roosevelt delivered a speech at Barnesville, Georgia, in August, 1938, charging that Senator Walter George could not possibly be classified "as belonging to the liberal school of thought." He had an understanding very different from that of Senator George as to what was required to get the country moving in the right direction again, and he chose to render those differences less complicated, as far as the electorate was concerned, by calling the senator "a dyed-in-the-wool conservative."[3]

The day after the President's attack on Senator George, a *New York Times* editorial came to the latter's defense by publishing his voting record on New Deal measures back to 1933. The editorial came to the following conclusions: that Senator George generally supported the purposes and methods of the Roosevelt administration, that he had differed with that administration on "comparatively few matters," and that the President required a great deal of "intellectual servitude" on the part of his party membership.[4] By citing Senator George's voting record all the way back to 1933, however, the editorial tended to obscure the fact that there was a struggle going on in the Democratic party at the time of that writing that had not been going on earlier, and that this was the occasion for the intervention on the part of the President. A month later, Turner Catledge reported, again in the *New York Times*, that

> basic to the whole trouble with the Democratic party is the fact that

> the old-time leaders, in Congress, were never devotees of what now have emerged as the principles of the New Deal. They followed along, and even led, in those days of 1933, 1934, 1935 and even 1936, under the assumption that the stress of the times would pass and the party would revert eventually to their care. However, following the 1936 election it became evident that the [New Deal program] was not to be wholly, or even primarily, an accumulation of emergency policies. It aimed at permanent readjustment of a nature which many of the old leaders had not contemplated.[5]

The *Times* editorial cites Senator George's voting record in 1937—that he supported three administration measures and opposed the same number—as evidence of his loyalty to the Democratic party. The three he supported, however, were the extension of the Reciprocal Tariff Act, continuation of the lending powers of the RFC, and an appropriation for the beginning of construction of the Gilbertsville Dam in the Tennessee Valley System, whereas the three he opposed were the court reform bill, the wages and hours bill, and the Wagner housing bill, all of which were extremely important parts of the administration's legislative program for that year. In evaluating the senator's loyalty to the party, in other words, the editorial fails to distinguish between bills of ordinary importance and those of paramount importance. In 1938, the editorial indicates that the senator supported the administration's "pump-priming" plan, its crop control plan, and new taxes for raising money for the payment of farm bounties, while he opposed the government reorganization bill. All in all, during the 1937–1938 period, Senator George opposed the following pieces of major New Deal legislation: the court reform bill, the wages and hours bill, the housing bill, and the government reorganization bill; and he supported the relief-recovery bill and the crop-control bill. Roosevelt suggested in his Barnesville speech that the test of party loyalty, in the case of an individual, is not "his every vote on *every* bill—of course not. The test lies rather in the answer to two questions: first, has the record of the candidate shown, while differing perhaps in details, a constant active fighting attitude in favor of the broad objectives of the party and of the Government as they are constituted today; and, secondly, does the candidate really, in his heart, deep in his heart, believe in those objectives?"[6] The fact was that the Senator had *not* after 1936 generally supported the broad objectives of the New Deal administration,[7] nor was he in fundamental harmony with those objectives.

The purge was unsuccessful in preventing the nomination of a number of anti–New Deal Democrats in the party primaries (for only Representative O'Connor was defeated in New York), but it provided that needed statement of purpose at the needed time which was to have broad political consequences for the Democratic party as a whole. The term "liberalism" is now so much a part of our political vocabulary that we are apt to forget that its usage is relatively recent as far as American politics is concerned. As a matter of fact, it came into vogue in the period of the Great Depression and was resuscitated at that time by FDR in the 1938 party primaries to describe the direction of his policies and the slant of his mind. In a letter written to Mrs. Mabel Walker Willebrandt on September 8, 1938, Roosevelt referred to his "effort at the very difficult task of interpreting in words, 'liberalism' and 'conservatism.' "[8] The political terms then current were "progressivism" and "conservatism." Roosevelt imparted to the term "liberalism" the notion of the major use of governmental power to regulate the economy. In progressivism, the desired relationship between the government and the economy had been that of improving private competition or freedom of competition but not regulation of many of the processes of the economy. There was the ill-defined recognition that some regulation was necessary and proper, but no principle was stated. In the New Deal, on the other hand, there was a principle stated that the national government must undertake responsibility, through its regulation, for the amelioration of the economy as a whole. The New Deal liberally used the commerce and taxing and spending powers of the national government to regulate the economy.

It certainly seems as if the American political system is at the present time very largely dependent upon party organizations or machines. The President was acutely aware, however, of the limitations on the extent to which his purposes could be achieved through the mechanism of party government. The purge has been explained as an attempt to drive conservative Democrats out of the party in Congress and to replace them with New Deal supporters, which was obviously true. But we must emphasize the fact that Roosevelt was more interested in the re-creation of the meaning of the Democratic party in

1938 than in its reogranization. FDR understood and believed in party organization, but only as an instrument through which to achieve party aims and purposes within the context of governing the nation.[9] In fact, the administrative reforms he advocated in the government reorganization bill were intended to help him govern the nation in the *absence* of strong party government. That bill, with the power given to the President to rearrange executive agencies and bureaus, would tighten the whole loosely organized structure of the national government and thus enable him to make more use of his position as head of the whole nation rather than as merely head of the party governing the nation.

Jim Farley described the President's intervention in the primaries as an attempt on the latter's part to establish a "personal" party, for he (Farley) conceived of the Democratic party as little more than an organization.[10] He failed to recognize that parties require principles or doctrines as well as organizations, that is, that interests cannot be held together indefinitely if they are not held together by a principle. The Democratic party boss, having no strong principled commitment to the New Deal, wrongly supposed that Roosevelt's action would weaken the party. It is not so surprising that Farley took such a narrow view, but it is surprising that that view is so widely shared by political scientists and historians.[11] We would like to suggest that Roosevelt's action settled once and for all the question of what the Democratic party was going to be like in the future, for prior to that time (and as far back as the end of the Civil War) that party had had difficulty being anything other than an organization. It had traditions, tendencies, and interests, but distinctive points of political doctrine were virtually nonexistent. The liberalism Roosevelt impressed upon the party in the 1938 primaries (which was predicated largely on a certain way of looking at the relationship between polity and economy) not only served to re-create the Democratic party, but, by virtue of that re-creation, it became the party that has initiated all the major legislative programs until very recent times.

Roosevelt's reconstituted liberalism, moreover, presented a choice to the electorate without being oblivious to the various groups and interests that make up that electorate. *His thinking about the Democratic party was principled without being doctrinaire.* He had no class notion of parties, no thoughts about proletarianizing the Democratic party in the image of the leading radical organization in the country. He believed that democratic institutions, properly ordered, necessitated political parties representing coalition majorities rather than fomenting a class struggle through remodeling the Democratic party along class lines. The New Deal, accordingly, consciously nourished the expansion of the middle class, which constituted a stabilizing and moderating force in American political life; for it tended to blur all distinctions of class without blurring all distinctions between interests.

The programs of the New Deal found their basis, we believe, in the Madisonian system. Roosevelt described that system as one "founded on the principle that many men from many states with many economic views and many economic interests might, through the medium of a national government, build for national harmony, national unity and independent well-being. . . . [The Madisonian system] means that government is intended to be the means by which all of these interests and policies are brought into equilibrium and harmony within a single Republic."[12]

Madison himself described that task in the following famous statement of *Federalist* ten: "The regulation of these various and interfering interests forms the principal task of modern legislation, and involves the spirit of party and faction in the necessary and ordinary operations of government." The New Deal may be understood as a new, vigorous application of this principle of regulation; that is, the function of government, as Roosevelt understood it, is in the spirit of that Madisonian principle. That principle consisted in reconciling the different claims of the different groups and interests in the community; but reconciliation, as he well knew, has its limits and a price, for the presence of the Southern faction in the Democratic coalition tended to weaken that coalition. Therefore, and of overriding importance, it is also the function of government to arrive at the common benefit or interest in which the rival claims of the different interests can be resolved (and that resolution may include the nullification of certain claims).[13] You cannot reconcile everyone. Every principle of reconciliation involves pleasing and offending certain groups, and in the case of the Democratic party the most offended group was the Southern faction. The particular resolution the New Deal achieved, which aimed at redistributing benefits among various groups and interests in the country, had a powerful moderating effect on that portion of the polity most susceptible to the attractions of a class orientation. But that resolution should not be confused with a consensus, for significant groupings within the Democratic party did not accede to the New Deal.

The significant resistance to social change during the depression came largely from within the Democratic party itself, for the opposition party was virtually defunct as a result of the overwhelming defeats it had suffered in the 1932 and 1936 presidential elections. What the purge accomplished was to separate or isolate that faction within the Democratic coalition most resistant to social change by reconstructing a liberalism on principles we can fairly identify as belonging to present-day liberalism. We will discuss in Chapter 9 how the New Deal shifted the emphasis of government from the pursuit of happiness to well-being, which was described by the President as the enlargement of the rights of the individual, or the actuality of his economic rights. The welfare state is a society in which happiness or well-being is no longer merely privately pursued; this means drastically expanded powers and responsibilities for the government generally. That reconstruction, therefore, involved a refurbishing of traditional liberalism through the infusion of Hamiltonianism (that is, broad national powers available for regulating the economy). By that reconstruction, the Democratic party revised the view it had of itself, and so did the nation. How the New Deal resolved the tensions between Hamiltonianism and Jeffersonianism in action may be suggested by Roosevelt's remark that "we have been trying . . . to make this nation conscious of the fact that it *is* a nation";[14] for, under the New Deal, the recourse to Hamiltonianism is what broadened the liberal perspective.

We have not refrained from using the harsh expression "purge," since it is helpful for rethinking the thoughts Roosevelt was thinking in 1938. In the 1938 purge, and even more in the New Deal taken as a whole, FDR was attempting to secure a settlement of one of the great divisive issues in American history: the relationship between government and the economy, and thereby that between government and the private life. His appraisal or transformation of the earlier liberalism may be taken to provide the justification for his own programs and policies, that is, instituting social welfare programs like Social Security which redistribute wealth, achieving a balance in the working of the national economy through regulatory measures of a fiscal and monetary nature, and revamping the structure of the national government. The ratification of this program would require the emergence of a party whose platform and leadership articulated the coming, if not the completed settlement, of that divisive issue. The emergence of such a party, however, demanded the elimination, or at least the exposure, of those members who rejected the new *raison d'être*. For only when a party emerged whose liberalism was pure (or purified) could there begin that further accommodation to the particular requirements of the circumstances which might have been expected from the New Deal itself. We would conclude that, despite the continued presence of dissident elements within the party after 1938, Roosevelt's identification of the Democratic party with his resolution of one of the divisive issues in American society permanently altered the balance of power in that party between liberals and "conservatives" and hence determined the kinds of policies and programs to be pursued by the party in the future. The subsequent apparent success of that party is the extent to which the programmatic aspirations of Roosevelt's New Deal have endured.

The term "purge" is not misleading as applied to the 1938 party primaries, since it means the separation of the bad from the good, and what FDR had in mind was a change in the principles of the Democratic party. In the immediate sense, the purge seems to have been a failure; Roosevelt did not succeed in cleansing the party of its most dissident elements. In the broad sense, however, of providing a formulation or definition of what the Democratic party was to stand for, the purge was a significant success.

CHAPTER 7

The Third-Term Issue

IN 1940, Roosevelt was faced with the supreme problem of his political career, that of deciding whether or not to run for a third term. The action whereby he provided for that decision should, therefore, be his most important action; for it was inextricably bound up with the preservation of the great gains of the New Deal as well as with the question of America's involvement in the European war. The things most important to the President at that time were providing for a continuity in administrations and the future handling of the nation's foreign policy. He would allow neither the two-term tradition nor the opposition of certain elements within his own party to stand in the way of these considerations. Roosevelt correctly saw that his possible withdrawal from a position of party leadership would increase the chances of a backsliding into conservative leadership on the national level. Moreover, the conservative faction in the Democratic party, led by Farley and Garner, was largely isolationist.

Roosevelt was the only American President ever elected to a third and even fourth term of office, thus shattering a tradition inaugurated by Washington. But in his Farewell Address in 1796, Washington almost apologized for his unwillingness to seek a third term, and the tradition can be more properly traced to Jefferson than to Washington. Now, of course, we have a Twenty-second Amendment to the Constitution intended to guarantee that this situation will not recur. The architects of that amendment believed that the presidency had become too powerful, and they feared an indefinitely strengthened presidency. Therefore, they saw in the amendment a way to cut the presidency down to size. The most serious criticism of that amendment is that it tends to weaken the President's authority within his own party during his second term in office, thus making it more difficult for him to ensure legislative support for his policies and programs. From the moment a President limited to two terms assumed office for a second time, he would cease to be a central personage in the American political system, for he would cease to have a vital function with regard to future legislation. It would not end his power altogether, but it would seriously weaken it. Roosevelt's willingness to break with the two-term tradition therefore calls our attention to the wrong-mindedness of that tradition.

What causes the greatest difficulty perhaps is understanding why FDR waited so long before indicating his willingness to run. He did not tell anyone what he was going to do until the very last moment. Therefore, his opponents were never quite sure whether he would run again or not, but there was no reason for assuming that he was practicing deception on the American people. He couldn't possibly reveal his intentions until the very last moment, for his influence at such a critical time in the history of our international relations would have been radically diminished the moment his retirement was announced. Contrariwise, any premature announcement of his intention to run again would have been equally disastrous, for those conservative Democrats who were reluctant to oppose Roosevelt as long as there was a chance of his withdrawal from a position of party leadership would abandon that reluctance once his decision to run again had become known. But as long as he kept everybody guessing, he could, as President, remain the only person capable of deciding the highest political questions. Ed Flynn, Farley's successor as national committee chairman, explained that "political skill is mostly built on proper timing. The correct time to announce a candidacy or the support of a particular candidate is as important as the announcement itself. If it is badly timed, the whole effect can be lost. . . . Should a man announce his candidacy too far in advance of a convention or primary, he can easily kill himself off through the opposition that will tend to develop and crystallize. Therefore, in practical politics an announcement is delayed as long as practicable, to prevent such a situation."[1] The President was in no great hurry to make his intentions known before it was absolutely necessary to do so; besides, for a very long time he didn't know just what his own intentions were.

His first mention of a third term occurred shortly after his second inauguration. In his Democratic Victory Dinner Address he said that it was his "ambition" to turn the presidential office over to his successor in 1941, but he did not say that he would necessarily do so. What would prevent his doing so would be the condition of the nation; that is to say, if the nation were not intact, not at peace, or not prosperous, he might feel obligated to seek another term. The telling remark in that address was: "I do not want to leave [the nation] to my successor in the condition in which Buchanan left it to Lincoln."[2] So Roosevelt does not meet the tradition's third-term prohibition squarely head on, but he meets the issue implicit in that prohibition. About two months later, at the same time the court-packing battle was raging, the President told three top congressional leaders—Joe Robinson, William B. Bankhead, and Sam Rayburn—that the court reform bill was at the top of his legislative "musts" and that, if they failed to secure its passage, he would be willing to take the issue to the electorate in 1938 or even in 1940. Alsop and Catledge reported that this intimation that the President *might* run again in 1940 upset these men a great deal.[3] It goes without saying that Roosevelt would have been a considerably weaker President for the remainder of his second term in office if the possibility of his candidacy had not been taken seriously, for every Democratic member of the Senate (including Robinson, Bankhead, and Rayburn) would know that they would never have to run for political office with this man again and that knowledge would be destructive of the President's political leadership. (One-third of the Senate would have to run for office while he was on the ticket seeking reelection). But because a President faces reelection, because of the possibility of his returning to political office, precisely for that reason, every day he is in office, he exerts a certain measure of control over his party. The impossibility of his reelection would tend to isolate him, to force him to withdraw, and entirely to weaken him.

The third-term controversy was rendered more bitter by the fact that many presidential ambitions were shattered as a result of the President's decision to run again, and a number of memoirs have been written which bear the telltale scars. Jim Farley, for example, has written that he might have been Vice-President or even President "had it not been for the man many have credited me with putting in the White House."[4] But Farley's downfall was brought about by Farley himself. That downfall could have been avoided, moreover, if he had been satisfied with the Democratic nomination for governor of New York; but he turned down Roosevelt's invitation to accept the gubernatorial nomination and so never really put himself in the position of being seriously considered for the presidential nomination. If he was unwilling to take on gubernatorial responsibilities in New York State (knowing full well that public criticism goes hand in hand with that kind of responsibility), how could anyone, including FDR, suppose that he would be any more vigorous in pursuing the responsibilities of the presidency? It seems that Garner had convinced him that Roosevelt was trying to get him out of the way as a presidential contender by coaxing him into the gubernatorial spot. But in view of the fact that the leadership of the largest and most important state in the nation would have given Farley the executive experience he sorely lacked, it appears that not FDR but Garner himself was trying to eliminate him, at least at that time, as a presidential candidate.

Farley was anxious to get the President to declare himself out of the running in 1939 because the latter stood in the way of his own ambitions, both presidential and vice-presidential. In other words, if Roosevelt ran, it would be highly unlikely that Farley could ever become the vice-presidential candidate, for they were both from the same state. But FDR never considered Farley as a possible successor and never encouraged him to seek the presidential nomination. He once remarked to Grace Tully that he "never heard Jim Farley make a constructive suggestion or even criticism regarding anything of importance to the country as a whole. He makes a routine report on the Post Office but has no idea of the broad objectives of this Administration."[5] Surely Farley should have had no delusions regarding his own capabilities as a political leader. He was not the master politician and leader that Roosevelt was, nor did he have the national following that Roosevelt had. But he simply refused to face the facts of political life, for, even after his refusal to run for governor of New York, he still expected the President not to stand in the way of his nomination.

It is merely reciting recent history to recall that the conservative attempt to stop Roosevelt from running for a third term—a movement instigated or at least encouraged by Vice-President

Garner—ended in failure. Roosevelt rightly counted on the collapse of the conservative opposition. In July, 1939, the Senate passed the Hatch bill, which was purportedly aimed at preventing federal officeholders from engaging in political activities, but was in fact intended to keep Roosevelt from controlling the 1940 Democratic convention. Moreover, this was the only piece of legislation the Vice-President had publicly endorsed. In the words of his biographer, Garner supported the Hatch bill because he thought it might prevent an "officeholders' oligarchy" from controlling presidential succession.[6] But organized labor's opposition to the Vice-President canceled him out as a real third-term threat. The complete collapse of the Garner movement was actually effected by the Wisconsin and Illinois primaries, in which he ran considerably behind the President. The Garner forces, at the time, agreed to abandon their "stop-Roosevelt" movement in return for the Vice-President's being allowed to keep the Texas delegation, thus reducing him to a "favorite-son" candidate. We believe it correct to say that, as long as Roosevelt remained in a position of party leadership as a potential third-term candidate, the cause of the conservatives was lost, for they could not even unite among themselves.

Although the two-term precedent originates with Washington, it is often overlooked that he was not in favor of any limitation on the number of terms a President should serve. In a letter to the Marquis de Lafayette, written in April, 1788, Washington said that he "differed widely" from both Jefferson and the Frenchman "as to the expediency or necessity of rotation" in the presidential office: "The matter was fairly discussed in the convention, and to my full conviction . . . there cannot in my judgment be the least danger, that the president will by any practical intrigue ever be able to continue himself one moment in office, much less perpetuate himself in it, but in the last stage of corrupted morals and depravity." Washington concluded by saying that he could see "no propriety in precluding ourselves from the services of any man, who on some great emergency shall be deemed universally most capable of serving the public."[7] The reason for the lack of restriction on the number of terms a President could serve in the American Constitution itself was to give the people the democratic opportunity to determine whether they wanted the man and his policies to continue or terminate.

Washington's correspondence, in the period between his retirement as commander in chief (or immediately prior to that retirement) and the meeting of the Constitutional Convention, reveals a man torn between two conflicting desires—the desire to retire from public life and the desire to see the new republican union established on firmer foundations. Even before he retired as commander in chief, and at the very time he was yearning for retirement, he wrote Hamilton in March, 1783: "My wish to see the union of these States established upon liberal and permanent principles, and inclination to contribute my mite in pointing out the defects of the present constitution, are equally great."[8] In a letter to Benjamin Harrison, dated January, 1784, he described himself as a private citizen who like them is subject to the evil consequences of a "half-starved, limping government, that appears to be always moving upon crutches and tottering at every step."[9] And in a letter to John Jay in August, 1786, the tension between these two opposing desires becomes most apparent: "I do not conceive, we can exist long as a nation, without lodging somewhere, a power which will pervade the whole Union in as energetic a manner, as the authority of the state governments extends over the several states. Retired as I am from the world, I frankly acknowledge I cannot feel myself an unconcerned spectator. Yet having happily assisted in bringing the ship into port, and having been fairly discharged, it is not my business to embark again on the sea of troubles."[10] The deciding factor in Washington's resolve to come out of retirement was his awareness of the need for reforming the Articles of Confederation. In the previously quoted letter to Harrison, he also said: "The disinclination of the individual States to yield competent powers to Congress for the federal government, their unreasonable jealousy of that body and of one another, and the disposition, which seems to pervade each, of being all-wise and all-powerful within itself, will, if there is not a change in the system, be our downfall as a nation. This is as clear to me as A, B, C."[11] It is hardly necessary to stress the fact that the two opposite motivations were joined in Washington's mind in an apparently impossible union.

In a speech delivered in April, 1939, Roosevelt indicated his understanding of why Washington had emerged from retirement to assume the presidential chair: "That Washington should have refused public service if the call had been a normal one has always been my belief. But the summons to the Presidency had come to him in a time of real crisis and deep emergency. The dangers that beset the young nation were as real as though the very independence that Washington had won for it had been threatened once more by foreign foes. Clear it must have been that the permanence of the Republic was at stake."[12] Roosevelt's situation in 1939 clearly reminded him of what had happened at the time when Washington made his decision to renew his political career.

As late as the spring of 1940, Roosevelt still had not definitely made up his mind as to whether or not he would run. In response to a plea from Dan Tobin of the Teamsters' Union that he should run again, the President, according to Labor Secretary Frances Perkins, replied as follows: "No, no, Dan. I just can't do it. I tell you, I have been here a long time. I am tired. I really am. You don't know what it's like. And besides, I have to take care of myself. . . . I have to get over this sinus. I have to have a rest. I want to go home to Hyde Park. I want to take care of my trees. I have a big planting there, Dan. I want to make the farm pay. I want to finish my little house on the hill. I want to write history. I just can't do it, Dan."[13] These remarks do not constitute a clear refusal to run again. It appears that the President is debating the question in his own mind, and it is only after a struggle within himself that he brings himself to seek renomination.

FDR was certainly aware of the difficulties involved in transgressing the tradition's third-term prohibition, for no American President before him had made the attempt and Jefferson had explicitly spoken out against it. The two-term tradition, moreover, was regarded by many as a safeguard to liberty. But all his past accomplishments might have been wasted if he had withdrawn from the national political scene in 1940, and hence created a vacuum in which the conservative element in the Democratic party could have reasserted itself. For, as was made abundantly clear by Roosevelt, you cannot expect lasting reforms in government like those instituted by the New Deal unless you have some reasonable assurance of continuity in administrations. The success of the New Deal in renovating American democratic institutions made it all the more imperative therefore that Roosevelt secure that continuity, even at the expense of breaking a time-honored tradition, for he knew that the old-line Democratic politicians would not be satisfied with anything less than the repeal of New Deal laws and the dissolution of its programs.

The most perplexing problem of Roosevelt's entire political career was his deciding whether or not to run for a third term. What he feared most was the possibility that, if he decided to retire from the national political scene, the succession might go by default into the hands of the conservatives. Well into 1940 he had not definitely made up his mind whether or not to run, and events in Europe played a crucial role in influencing his decision. But from 1937 on, he was determined not to close the door on a third term, for that would necessarily have destroyed his influence as a national as well as a party leader. One can easily receive the impression that, since FDR had not made up his own mind about running again, he made no attempt to groom a possible successor. His wife had written that she was "deeply troubled" by his failure to prepare a successor and she told him so. He replied that "he thought people had to prepare themselves, that all he could do was to give them opportunities and see how they worked out." After consideration, she admitted that she had finally come to realize that "this was something that people had had to do many times before and that no man could hand another more than opportunity."[14] It appears that Roosevelt's actual plan called for the building up of a number of potential candidates—Harry Hopkins, Paul V. McNutt, and Robert H. Jackson. Hopkins and McNutt were given appointments as secretary of commerce and federal security administrator respectively in order to enhance their prestige and allow public attitudes toward their candidacy to crystallize; and Roosevelt sought the gubernatorial nomination in New York for Jackson, but Farley prevented that. But the President would not help to build up a successor in whom he had no confidence—he would never have consented to Farley's succeeding him as leader of the Democratic party. And this does not contradict the fact that he had also urged Farley to run for governor of New York.

Roosevelt's nomination in 1940 underscored the defeat of the defunct conservative element in the Democratic party. In fact, the conservatives couldn't even influence the vice-presidential nomination. Roosevelt's threat to decline the presidential nomination after it had been tendered, if Henry Wallace wasn't approved as his running mate, took the conservative

Democrats by surprise and trapped them into acquiescing in something to which they otherwise would never have agreed. Roosevelt was simply unwilling to compromise on the choice of a presidential successor in the case of his own death at such a critical time in the nation's history. He explained to Farley that he chose Wallace because, if he died suddenly or was assassinated, he would want someone to carry on whom he could really depend upon to advance the best interests of the country in domestic and international affairs.[15] He did, of course, accept Harry S. Truman as a concession to party wishes four years later, but by that time his confidence in Wallace was shaken and the direction the nation was to take with regard to the European war was no longer an issue as it had been in 1940. The year 1940 was a time when the nation was split by differences of belief on how to deal with German and Japanese imperialism.

The United States in 1939 was necessarily heavily involved in international politics, that is, heavily committed to the cause of England and France, which made eventual American participation in the European war a real possibility. (Roosevelt became convinced that a foreign policy limited to preservation was impossible—contrary to the isolationist assertion that America could protect herself and her interests adequately without becoming intimately involved in international politics and its machinations.) As a matter of fact, Roosevelt had become deeply concerned with the problems of international politics by 1938, and his speeches after the Munich Conference reveal how quickly and how completely his emphasis shifted from domestic reform to foreign affairs. When Germany demanded the Sudetenland from Czechoslovakia as the price of peace, the order of emphasis was reversed. In his annual message to Congress in January, 1939, the President stated that the nation had "now passed the period of internal conflict in the launching of [its] program of social reform. . . . Events abroad had made it increasingly clear to the American people that dangers within are less to be feared than dangers from without."[16] Roosevelt looked at the massive dangers threatening the United States from Germany and Japan and was worried lest the foreign policy of the country be left in inexperienced hands. At the time of the Democratic convention in 1940, the *New York Times* editorialized that there were plenty of experienced men in the Democratic party who were capable of providing the nation with the necessary leadership in foreign affairs, and that therefore there was no reason in the world why the President would need to run for a third term.[17] But the simple truth of the matter is that there was not a man of the depression generation who was the equal of FDR. There were certain individuals who might be considered equals at first glance, such as Harry Hopkins, Harold Ickes, and Robert H. Jackson. But all these men, and all the others, too, were men of lesser stature.

In 1939, Roosevelt was beset by fears—the possibility of a victorious Germany, the possibility of a hostile Russia permanently aligned with Germany, the possibility of control over the government in Washington reverting to the conservative element in 1941—fears he constantly sought to combat. But the Roosevelt who confronts us in 1939 is not the statesman at the end of his political career, for he had not yet accomplished all he had to do. He saw his responsibilities at that time as those of preserving the great gains of the New Deal and, at the same time, overcoming the forces of isolationism that were so powerful in the country. But he surely was not worried about the third term as a matter of principle, for he seemed well satisfied that the broadest national interests could be served by *not* "changing horses in the middle of the stream." Alexander Hamilton defined this problem with mathematical precision, arguing that continuity and stability sometimes require tolerating the same hands for a long period of time:

> There is no nation which has not at one period or another experienced an absolute necessity of the service of particular men, in particular situations, perhaps it would not be too strong to say, to the preservation of its political existence. How unwise therefore must be every such self-denying ordinance, as serves to prohibit a nation from making use of its own citizens, in the manner best suited to its exigencies and circumstances. Without supposing the personal essentiality of the man, it is evident that a change of the chief magistrate, at the breaking out of a war, or at any similar crisis, for another even of equal merit, would at all times be detrimental to the community; inasmuch as it would substitute inexperience to experience and would tend to unhinge and set afloat the already settled train of the administration.[18]

Prior to the passage of the Twenty-second Amendment we had the right of the people to elect whomever they pleased, the possibility of perpetuating the best-qualified man in office, and a strong moral tradition of making it probably (but not necessarily) only two terms.

CHAPTER 8

For the National Defense: The Diplomacy of the Yalta Conference

ROOSEVELT'S New Deal was concerned primarily with the inner structure of the political community and not the external relations of the political community. Therefore a discussion of the Yalta Conference may seem somewhat out of place in a book that purports to deal with the contribution of the New Deal to American political thought and practice. But the largest problems of society, like those of war and peace, are surely political problems; and the way in which they are handled very often depends on the character of the society confronting those problems, not to mention the character of its political leaders. Consider, for example, the problem of dealing with the report of an imminent Japanese attack. The following story is reported by John Toland: "After reading the secretly decoded Japanese message on the night of December 6, Roosevelt said, 'This means war.' And then Harry Hopkins said, 'Since war is undoubtedly going to come at the convenience of the Japanese, it's too bad we can't strike the first blow.' Roosevelt replied, 'No, we can't do that. We are a democracy and a peaceful people.' "[1]

The agreements and understandings of the Yalta Conference concluded in February, 1945, represented the supreme effort of Roosevelt and his advisors to secure Soviet cooperation for establishing democratic governments in Eastern Europe, for they believed that it was possible to work together with the Russians within the framework of an international organization as an alternative to relying on spheres of influence. But the Soviet Union installed a Communist-controlled government in Rumania, in violation of the Declaration of Liberated Europe, only a few weeks after the signing of that declaration.

Secretary of War Henry Stimson has written that the conference dealt "a good deal in altruism and idealism instead of stark realities."[2] However this may be, the fact that the conference as a whole dealt with problems related to both war and peace (and therefore the coming into being of the peace) makes it possible for us to study the manner in which Roosevelt, one of the principal architects of the agreements arrived at there, sought to achieve peace and freedom. Yalta, moreover, has some affinity to the Cold War, for the issues left unsettled there became the burning issues of the Cold War period.

The Yalta Agreement has come to be associated in the public mind with secret and somehow shameful agreements. And some of the President's critics have had no difficulty in seeing that that part of the agreement made in secret by Roosevelt and Stalin contributed to the collapse of the Nationalist regime in China. Churchill signed the secret agreement along with Roosevelt and Stalin, but was careful to disassociate himself from it. He stated in his memoirs that "it was regarded as an American affair and was certainly of prime interest to their military operations. It was not for us to claim to shape it."[3] But, as Anthony Eden relates, Churchill insisted on signing it, for otherwise it might prevent the British from being party to later discussions on the Far East.[4] This agreement provided for Soviet participation in the Japanese war two or three months after the end of the war in Europe if the following conditions were met: (1) cession of the Kurile Islands and southern Sakhalin to the Soviet Union; (2) internationalization of the port of Dairen in Manchuria, with recognition of Soviet "preeminent interests" there; (3) restoration to the Soviet Union of the lease of Port Arthur as a naval base; (4) joint Chinese-Soviet operation of the Chinese-Eastern and South Manchurian railroads, with recognition of Soviet "preeminent interests" there; and (5) recognition of the status quo in Outer Mongolia. William C. Bullitt, who had been American ambassador to Russia and France, later wrote that "no more unnecessary, disgraceful and potentially dangerous document has ever been signed by a President of the United States."[5] And General Patrick J. Hurley, Roosevelt's wartime ambassador to China, has charged that "it surrendered the territorial integrity and political independence of China."[6] But it never has been established that this agreement brought about the collapse of the Nationalist regime in China. Nationalist China collapsed under its own weight.

In his study of the Second World War, Chester Wilmot considered it particularly unfortunate that FDR "volunteered" at the Teheran Conference in November, 1943, to restore Russia's rights in the Manchurian port of Dairen and hence assure her access to warm waters. Presumably this offer was made in return for Russia's coming into the Japanese war which, if we are able to accept the statement of Cordell Hull on its face, had already been promised by Stalin with no strings attached. And Stalin, says Wilmot, immediately saw Roosevelt as a "soft touch."[7] But Churchill wrote in his memoirs that it was he and not Roosevelt who first discussed the possibility with Stalin of Russia's having a warm-water port in the Pacific. Churchill says that Stalin brought up the matter and he expressed sympathy for Russia's desire because the future world must be entrusted to "satisfied nations" that want nothing more for themselves than what they already have. The future world, he continued, would hold much danger if it were in the hands of "hungry nations."[8] It was during this discussion that Roosevelt suggested Dairen, an ice-free harbor in southern Manchuria, as a possibility, but only as a free port under the control of an international commission. The establishment of free ports, as Sumner Welles points out, was always one of the President's favorite formulas for settling the status of localities where international controversies threatened to arise.[9]

The American Joint Chiefs of Staff consistently took the position until five months after Yalta that Soviet participation in the Japanese war was essential to the successful invasion of Japan with minimum losses. From the point of view of the American military planners, the logic of the war against Japan required the use of Soviet divisions against the Japanese in Manchuria while the American forces carried out a progressive invasion of the Japanese home islands. But Admiral William D. Leahy, the President's personal chief of staff, was opposed to this strategy, arguing that the continuation of the naval and air blockade would sooner or later bring about Japan's surrender without the need for an actual invasion. However, the Joint Chiefs insisted that we must have the use of Soviet divisions in Manchuria, which, as George F. Kennan indicates, implied the Soviet occupation of Manchuria.[10] The United States could not escape the political risks that would be incurred if the Soviets carried on full-scale military operations in Manchuria. It would place them in full military control of the country and its railroads, and hence give them a tremendous influence in Chinese internal politics. There are indeed situations in which a nation has to take calculated political risks for the sake of the greatest possible military advantage. In this situation, FDR had to weigh the risk of Russia's presence in Manchuria against the greater possible advantage of diverting a powerful Japanese army during an anticipated invasion of the Japanese home islands. The Far Eastern Agreement was negotiated as a matter of paramount military necessity. Yalta was still a wartime conference, and no one could actually foresee when and how the end of the Japanese war would come about.

But it ought to be perfectly obvious that the Russians would have expected the restoration of rights formerly held in Manchuria if they were asked to participate in the war in Manchuria. It was Russia that, prior to the Russo-Japanese war, had built the Chinese-Eastern Railroad across northern Manchuria to connect with the line to Vladivostok and was completing construction of a branch of that railroad through southern Manchuria from Harbin to Port Arthur and Dairen. By the Treaty of Portsmouth in 1905, a victorious Japan took over the southern branch of that railroad (in addition to Port Arthur and Dairen); and in 1935, after the invasion of northern Manchuria by the Japanese, the Russians were forced to sell the Chinese-Eastern to the Japanese puppet government there. Stalin's promise to Cordell Hull of Russian participation in the Japanese war presumably with no strings attached must be taken with a grain of salt. In his conversations with Hull, Stalin never excluded the possibility of asking for concessions when the Japanese war would reach that stage of actually requiring Russian intervention. Therefore that promise was exaggerated.

Wilmot contends that the real issue of Yalta for the world and for the future was not what Stalin would or could have taken there, but what he was given the right to take. He looks upon the Far Eastern agreement as a "green light" given to Stalin to take whatever he wanted in Eastern Europe. And, more particularly, Roosevelt was not well placed to defend the sovereignty of Poland, says Wilmot, once he had agreed to the infringement of China's sovereignty without her consent.[11] But FDR did not give Stalin the right to take anything in Eastern Europe, Poland included. It was the Declaration of Liberated Europe in particular that was intended to deprive of legal justification whatever expansionist ambitions Stalin had for Eastern Europe. If anyone made it possible for the Russians to establish their claims in Eastern Europe, it was the British and not FDR. It is not necessary to repeat here the details of the Russo-British sphere-of-influence agreements of 1944. It suffices to say that Churchill and Stalin agreed that the controlling influence in Rumania and Bulgaria would be exercised by the Soviet Union; in Greece, by Great Britain; and in Yugoslavia and Hungary, equally by the two powers. In defending these agreements, Churchill wrote his cabinet colleagues in London that it is easy to see that the Soviet Union has "vital interests" in the countries bordering on the Black Sea, by one of whom, Bulgaria, it had been attacked, and with the other of whom, Rumania, it has ancient ties.[12] But once he had agreed to an arrangement over Eastern Europe, Churchill was not well placed to defend the sovereignty of Rumania after the Soviet coup there in February, 1945, for, as he later stated, Stalin would then remind him of Soviet respect for British predominance in Greece.[13]

It was the precise intention of the Declaration of Liberated Europe to disestablish any claims the Russians might have had to Eastern Europe as a result of the sphere-of-influence agreements of the previous year. That Declaration outlined a procedure for the liberated countries of Eastern Europe which contemplated the formation of provisional governments broadly representative of all nonfascist elements in the population and committed to the earliest possible establishment through free elections of governments responsive to the will of the people. Without a doubt, the sphere-of-influence agreements, establishing Soviet preeminence in Rumania and Bulgaria, were regarded by the Soviets as a formal acknowledgment of their continuing predominance in that area. What FDR refused to concede at Yalta was the division of Eastern Europe into spheres of influence, for he looked forward to the setting up of popular governments in that part of the world. Before leaving for Yalta, he indicated to the Congress that "in the future world the misuse of power, as implied in the term 'power politics,' must not be a controlling factor in international relations. . . . We cannot deny that power is a factor in world politics any more than we can deny its existence as a factor in national politics. But in a democratic world, as in a Democratic Nation, power must be linked with responsibility, and obliged to justify itself within the framework of a general good."[14] The linking together of power and responsibility, or the responsible exercise of power, directed toward ends consistent with the well-being of international society, as Roosevelt believed, set the tone for postwar international relations. It pointed therefore to a working international organization that would reduce the necessity for relying upon spheres of influence.

It makes no sense to say, as Wilmot does, that Roosevelt was not well placed to defend the sovereignty of Poland once concessions had been made to the Soviets over Manchuria. Poland's sovereignty had already been compromised before the Yalta Conference ever convened by the presence of Soviet forces in that country and the installation of the Soviet-sponsored Lublin Committee as the provisional government of Poland. What had led to the emergence of the Lublin regime was the breakdown in negotiations between the Soviets and the exiled Polish government in London in November, 1944, and the resignation of Stanislaw Mikolajczyk as head of that government. The basic disagreement between Stalin and the London Poles was over the eastern boundary of postwar Poland. Stalin was absolutely insistent and Churchill had agreed that the Curzon Line should become the new boundary between Poland and the Soviet Union, which would give eastern Poland to the latter. Churchill told the House of Commons, not long after Teheran, that he thought the Russian demand did not exceed "the limits of what was reasonable and just."[15] However, despite continuous efforts by the British to bring the London Poles around, the cession of eastern Poland was absolutely unacceptable to them. Stalin would have been willing in October, 1944, to consent to Mikolajczyk as prime minister of a provisional government provided, first, that the Curzon Line would be acceptable to the London Poles as the eastern boundary of Poland and, second, that the Lublin Poles would have a majority of ministers in the new government. When Mikolajczyk hesitated, Churchill made it clear to him that the British were committed to the Curzon Line as the basis for a settlement and that this was no time for the London Poles and the British to separate on this issue.[16] Churchill was "more interested in the question of Poland's sovereign independence and freedom than in particular frontier lines," as he later remarked, while Mikolajczyk believed that the "question of frontiers and independence closely intertwine."[17] A Poland that was forced to surrender its eastern half to the Soviet Union, the latter reasoned, would necessarily become a Soviet satellite. Mikolajczyk finally did agree to ask his ministers in London to accept the Stalin proposals, but they refused, an action that resulted in his resignation. Stalin thereupon took advantage of his resignation to recognize the Lublin Committee as the provisional government of Poland.

After returning from the October conference with Stalin, Churchill told the Commons that "if the Polish Government had taken the advice we tendered them at the beginning of the year, the additional complication produced by the formation of the Polish National Committee at Lublin would not have arisen."[18] By refusing to acquiesce to Stalin's demands, the London Poles were seen by Churchill to have disregarded their own interests or to have acted irrationally, for, as he believed, the "additional complication" of the Lublin regime could have been avoided. He belived that if the London Poles had been willing to agree to the Curzon Line, Stalin could have been persuaded to permit the establishment of a free and independent Poland. The Prime Minister, having wholly overlooked the novelty of Soviet imperialism, only became worried about Soviet intentions regarding the whole of Poland after it became obvious that Stalin was going to recognize the Lublin regime. But nothing could restore relations between the London Poles and the Soviet Union since the former would never willingly have conceded the surrender of eastern Poland. It was therefore in the cards that Stalin would turn to another Polish regime.

Nevertheless, it was agreed at Yalta to concentrate on creating a coalition out of the Lublin and London groups to govern Poland during an interim period before free elections could be held, and it was further agreed that to this end the Lublin regime should be reorganized to include other democratic elements from Poland and abroad. In other words, a reorganized and not an enlarged Lublin regime was agreed upon at Yalta as the basis for a new provisional government. Still, it was to be a reorganized *Lublin* regime and not a reconstituted Polish regime, which means that the Polish Communists already had the decisive advantage. Eden knew before Yalta what Churchill should have known—that "the time has probably gone by for a 'fusion' of London and Lublin."[19] Therefore it is hard to see what Polish sovereignty there was for Roosevelt to compromise during or after the Yalta Conference. Churchill had simply failed in 1944 to withstand Stalin's efforts to create a Communist Poland.

Shortly after Yalta, Churchill assured the Commons that Stalin had made "most solemn declarations" that the sovereign independence of Poland would be maintained: "I feel . . . that their word is their bond. I know of no government which stands to its obligations, even in its own despite, more solidly than the Russian Soviet Government. I decline absolutely to embark here on a discussion of Russian good faith. Somber indeed would be the fortunes of mankind if some awful schism arose between the Western Democracies and the Russian Soviet Union. We are now entering a world of imponderables, and at every stage occasions for self-questioning arise. Only one link in the chain of destiny can be handled at a time."[20] We cannot be guided by considerations of an unknown future, the prime minister intimated, but only by what we can now know and foresee. However, that very same evening, the Soviet deputy foreign minister, Andrei Vishinsky, demanded the dismissal of the Radescu government in Rumania and the formation of a new government headed by a pro-Communist in violation of the Declaration of Liberated Europe. Churchill made no protest against the Soviet move; for, as he later explained, he did not want to do anything that might harm the chances of securing a genuinely reconstituted Polish government, over and above the fact that the sphere-of-influence agreements of the previous year had given the Soviets a predominance in Rumania.[21] But Molotov was soon arguing that little more than an enlarged Lublin regime was all that was ever intended at Yalta. It was no surprise therefore that when the composition of the new provisional government was announced on June 28 by a Polish round-table conference convened in Moscow, sixteen of the twenty-one new ministers had been former members of the Lublin regime and only five were from the outside. But without even waiting for the agreed reorganization to take place, Stalin had negotiated a treaty of mutual assistance with the Lublin regime on April 21, an action that was contrary to the spirit of the Polish accord.

The whole of Churchill's argument in the Commons in

defense of the Polish accord was based on the absolute necessity of trust, trust in solemn promises. Without trust, nations cannot exist, and Churchill and FDR were willing to gamble on Russian good faith. The Yalta Agreement would not have been worth the signing if the parties to that agreement could not be presumed to abide by its stipulations. The presumption that the Russians would live up to their promises was based in part on an estimate of their past performance. But Stalin never kept the solemn promises he made at Yalta, thus indicating the extent to which that trust had been misplaced.

It will be recalled that the Yalta Conference was FDR's last conference and therefore the one in which he went furthest toward defining the peace. However, the matter of the indefinite continuation of British, French, and Dutch colonial possessions in the Far East, a matter that was to have a far-reaching effect on the character of the peace, was never discussed there. Its mere suggestion in the form of a proposal for a trusteeship council in the new international organization brought an explosive reaction from Churchill, who said that under no circumstances would he ever consent to forty or fifty nations thrusting their "interfering fingers" in the very existence of the British Empire.[22] But as early as September, 1943, FDR envisioned full partnership for Indonesia in the Netherlands federation and the severence of Indo-China from French control with the establishment of a trusteeship there in which the Philippines would play a major role.[23] He had suggested at Teheran that the future world organization should manage "trusteeships" for former dependencies with a view to their securing independence as soon as possible. And he was determined that Indo-China in particular should not be returned to France, but that it should be administered by an international trusteeship.[24] FDR saw the greatest danger to future peace in colonialism. He said to his son Elliot that "the colonial system means war. Exploit the resources of an India, a Burma, a Java: take all the wealth out of those countries, but never put anything back into them, things like education, decent standards of living, minimum health requirements—all you're doing is storing up the kind of trouble that leads to war. All you're doing is negotiating the value of any kind of organizational structure for peace before it begins."[25] But he would have been very wrong to believe, and we do not think he did believe, that there was a British and French and Dutch colonialism but that there could be no Russian colonialism.

During the Atlantic Charter Conference in 1941, the President told Churchill that "the peace cannot include any continued despotism. The structure of the peace demands and will get equality of peoples."[26] Roosevelt knew that peace is always with a view to something else. He understood that freedom (that is, the limited or ordered freedom of a free society) was an end more final than peace and that the intrinsic value of peace derives from the freedom it achieves. And the colonial system is the very antithesis of freedom. We would suggest that FDR looked forward to an international organization that would reinforce the structure of the peace by converting colonies into "trusteeships" on their way to self-government and self-sufficiency. He viewed the mechanism of trusteeship as a way of implementing point three of the Atlantic Charter, which speaks of the necessity for all people to choose the form of government under which they should live. But Churchill maintained that point three of the Charter applied only to the occupied countries of Europe and not to Asia. He was thinking of India and Burma in particular.

It would seem that the characteristic difference between Churchill and FDR was that the latter viewed the aspirations and grievances of the peoples of the colonial and semicolonial areas of the world as the massive political problem of the emerging democratic world and Churchill did not, however great the prime minister's other merits may have been. And it was precisely for this reason, as Roosevelt believed, that the restoration of the peace should include the removal of colonialism. That removal would help prevent colonial revolutions from becoming Communist revolutions. He envisioned the end of colonialism and the emergence of the underdeveloped nations into full development or, as its alternative, a civil-war-of-the-whole-world. Surely the removal of colonialism does not guarantee the wise use or preservation of freedom, as nothing is more inimical to freedom than an experiment in democracy before the necessary preconditions have been fulfilled. Roosevelt knew that political freedom cannot be appropriated without any intellectual and moral effort whatsoever. But the mechanism of trusteeship was a surer way, he believed, to the eventual exercise of the responsibilities of freedom than the indefinite continuation of the colonial system.

The Yalta Conference was the climactic conference of the Second World War in the sense that it was the last conference in which the three great war leaders participated together. Moreover, that conference stood between war and peace, and therefore was characterized by the interplay between war and peace. As Roosevelt remarked before leaving for that conference: "Many of the problems of the peace are upon us even now while the conclusion of the war is still before us."[28] The most urgent problem of the peace under discussion there was, in his opinion, the status of the former independent states of Eastern Europe whose future was spelled out in the Declaration of Liberated Europe. The President was willing to make concessions to Stalin that were tantamount to restoring to the Soviet Union a sphere of influence in Manchuria[29] for considerations of military necessity. But he would make no concessions that involved the dividing up of Eastern Europe into spheres of influence, for he was concerned above all else with securing world freedom within the framework of an international organization comprising many or all nations. Churchill's percentage agreements with Stalin in 1944, moreover, represented to Roosevelt an approach to international problems hardly compatible with the principles of the Atlantic Charter or the United Nations Declaration.

The lesson of Yalta is that it draws our attention most forcefully to the limitations of treaties and covenants as instruments of accommodation among nations. It is therefore necessary to understand that the keeping of treaties and covenants presupposes a measure of trustworthiness which was evidently lacking in the Yalta councils. When Churchill made the suggestion at that conference that the great powers establish an interim government for the Poles then and there until such time as the Polish people could form their own government, Stalin replied that he had enough "democratic feeling" in him to refuse to create a Polish government without the consent of the Poles themselves.[30] But he never had any intention of allowing the Poles to govern themselves. It seems that neither Churchill nor FDR had given sufficient consideration to the precarious nature of their relationship with the calculating Stalin. They had taken his trustworthiness too much for granted. We thus arrive at the conclusion that the Yalta Agreement was not the wisest agreement ever negotiated; but that FDR behaved much more wisely under the circumstances than he is given credit for, and certainly no less prudently and realistically than Churchill with all his talk about the "vital interests" of the Soviet Union in Eastern Europe and the reasonableness and justice of their claims.

CHAPTER 9

For the General Welfare: The New Deal and the Welfare State

THE American political tradition is ordinarily understood to have a liberal character, but that part of the tradition represented by Roosevelt and the New Deal is definitely not that of the earlier liberalism. We would suggest that the full measure and meaning of our liberal democratic tradition cannot be understood without an understanding of the essential changes that have occurred within the framework of that tradition and that have altered the course of that tradition. For this purpose, it is helpful to observe that the main thrust of the opposition to the New Deal in the second Roosevelt administration took the form of opposition within the Congress to crucial pieces of New Deal legislation like the low cost housing and slum clearance bill, the wages and hours bill, and the government reorganization bill. By examining the views of some of the more outspoken opponents of these measures, we can discern several distinct but related kinds of argument that help to characterize the earlier liberalism. We are concerned primarily, however, with the way in which FDR's manner of looking at questions about the common good marks the limits of the earlier liberalism by transcending it in the direction of the welfare state.

As we have indicated, one of the divisive political issues in the Seventy-fifth Congress was that of low-cost housing and slum clearance. The advocates of the bill believed that the potentialities of individuals could not be realized because of the slums in which they lived. They argued that putting families in better living quarters and eliminating slums tend to emancipate the initiative and talents of individuals and enable the country to become more prosperous and enlightened. The whole housing and slum clearance program was understood as a nation-building project. But it is impossible to allocate funds from the federal treasury, to which the whole country contributes, without spending it in certain parts of the country, where some particular individuals and groups would derive particular advantages. As Senator Tydings of Maryland, one of the critics of the bill, stated: "[I] predict that New York will receive practically all the money that this bill contains. I make the prediction that with this bill in its present form, at least half of the money will find its way into New York City or the immediately surrounding area and that the municipality will not put up a red penny."[1] From this statement we can understand why Senator Carter Glass of Virginia, another critic of the bill, argued that Congress had no authority to confer economic benefits that were not simultaneously enjoyed by *all* the American people. He demanded to know "upon what recognized theory of government it ever became the business of the National Government here in Washington to tax all the American people to clear up slums in certain specified parts of the country."[2] The characteristic New Deal answer, as stated by the President, was that the improvement of the part was simultaneously the improvement of the whole, for an interdependence existed in the country which made the disease of slums a national concern.[3] In other words, slums and slum housing, while local in their existence, are national in their effects.

The critics of the wages and hours bill saw that the power to be given the wage board in Washington was much more than the power simply to deal with wages and hours. It became, in their view, a power involving life and death over all the industry and all the labor in the country. Behind the opposition to this bill, of course, was the fact that the comparatively low wages upon which Southern industries had been developed so recently could not be raised without forcing many of these industries to the wall and therefore diminishing available opportunities for employment in the South.[4] Senator Walter F. George of Georgia, who in 1938 described himself as a "liberal, but a liberal within the Constitution," denounced the proposed legislation as "bureaucracy run mad" and "the wildest dream that was ever presented to the American Congress." He characterized it as an attempt on the part of sinister Washington cabals to establish centralization in America:

Back of this thing stands the almost undisguised purpose of putting into the hands of a board at Washington all the industry, all the labor in America, with all its political and economic consequences.... [There are unmistakable signs] of an intent to bring under Washington, with vast power, virtually unrestricted and unrestrained, the great populations in the industrial and commercial centers.... I have seen in it the possibility at least of controlling America through a group of industrial and commercial cities in America, and not the least effective means of control will be agencies at Washington which possess a power which never should be vested in any board or any bureau, or delegated by any Congress.[5]

The wage board implements the task of regulating the economic life of the nation, the reasoning runs, and therefore contributes to the concentration of power in the hands of the urban industrial and financial interests, without a concern for the needs of the rest of the country. No individual or group is wise enough, moreover, to give the rule for an entire national economy.

The opponents of the government reorganization bill emphasized that giving the President virtual unconditional authority to merge or abolish executive agencies would mean the increased concentration of power in and the excessive growth of the administrative or executive branch of the government. They further argued that this proliferation of bureaucracy, by implementing the task of regulating economic life, threatens democracy in that it narrows down the individual's freedom to manage his own affairs. This is the meaning of Senator Borah's remark that "bureaucracy is the *disease* of government, and there is no instance on record in which any government has ever found a cure for it. It attaches itself to all forms of government.... It has greater and more persistent staying power than government itself. The problem which confronts us is the restraining and controlling of the remarkable bureaucratic growth of this country. Burdensome to the taxpayer and destructive of democratic principles, bureaucracy means much more than a casual reading of the proposed bill would indicate."[6] Bureaucracy, as opposed to limited government with limited powers, was considered ultimately incompatible with democratic government in that it subverts democratic liberty. As Robert E. Sherwood, the Hopkins biographer, observed: "The cries of 'dictatorship' raised against Roosevelt's reorganization proposals were much the same as those raised by the enemies of ratification of the Constitution, except that then the scare word was 'monarchy.' "[7]

There seem to be three separate arguments here. The first is that problems like slum surroundings and inadequate housing are not national problems and that therefore legislation designed to alleviate these problems does not benefit the country as a whole but only a part of it. The point of view which guides this criticism is that the urban sections of the country would become the recipient of the lion's share of governmental spending. The second is that the authority granted a wage board in Washington to deal with wages and hours on a nationwide basis becomes a power involving life and death over all the industry and all the labor in the country, with all its centralizing consequences. And the third is that the power to rearrange executive agencies and bureaus and hence create new ones tends toward the dangerous concentration of power in the hands of the executive and the concomitant growth of an enormous, irresponsible bureaucracy. That the rearrangement of executive agencies and bureaus would tighten up the loosely organized structure of the American government is precisely what its critics feared. All these New Deal measures taken together, in the view of the earlier liberalism, have the tendency to produce centralization and bureaucracy, the diseases of modern democratic government.[8] Both centralization and bureaucracy were regarded as incompatible with our traditional democracy; for, under the circumstances of bureaucratic centralization, government could no longer remain responsive to the will of the electorate. The very existence of democracy itself, as conceived by the earlier liberalism, was held to depend upon the exemption of certain spheres of economic and social activity from the intrusion of big government.

It is an oversimplification of some convenience to say that the hostility of the earlier liberalism to the regulatory and welfare measures of the New Deal rested on a narrow understanding of the purpose of government. In a Labor Day statement to the American people in 1937, the President outlined his broadened understanding: "The Government has committed itself to a very definite program in the advancement of the economic, industrial and spiritual welfare of our people. . . . We have attempted to create work security with reasonable wages and humane conditions of employment; to provide better homes and bring the family life of our country new comforts and a greater happiness."[9] We must never forget that an important part of the earlier liberalism was the simple consideration that all the really important things in life are done by society, setting society apart from government, and that the function of government is primarily to secure the *conditions* of happiness. Perhaps its most important formulation occurs in Tom Paine's *The Rights of Man*:

> Government is no farther necessary than to supply the few cases to which society and civilization are not conveniently competent; and instances are not wanting to show, that everything that government can usually add thereto, has been performed by the common interest of society, without government. . . . It is but few general laws that civilized life requires, and those of such common usefulness, that whether they are enforced by the same forms of government or not, the effect will be nearly the same. If we consider what the principles are that first condense men into society, and what the motives that regulate their mutual intercourse afterwards, we shall find, by the time we arrive at what is called government, that nearly the whole of the business [of government] is performed by the natural operation of the parts [of society] upon each other.[10]

The earlier liberalism held especially that government has the function of guaranteeing life, liberty, and the pursuit of happiness, but *not* the enjoyment or possession of happiness. The view that the happiness and well-being of the greater number should be provided for by government is, in modern terms, a welfare-state view; and it emerged in this country in the period of the Great Depression.

Roosevelt was undoubtedly right when he said that "heretofore, Government had merely been called upon to produce the *conditions* within which people could live happily, labor peacefully, and rest secure. Now it was called upon to [raise the standard of living for everyone; to bring luxury[11] within the reach of the humblest; . . . and to release everyone from the drudgery of the heaviest manual toil]."[12] He pointed out that "it is a relatively *new thing* in American life to consider what the relationship of Government is to its starving people and its unemployed citizens, and to take steps to fulfill its governmental duties to them. A generation ago people had scarcely given thought to the terms 'social security,' 'minimum wages,' or 'maximum hours.' "[13] The President most assuredly shared the earlier liberal view as far as it went, but he gave it a *new dimension* when he insisted that "all reasonable people must recognize that government was not intituted to serve as a cold public instrument to be called into use after irreparable damage has been done. If we limit government to functions of punishing the criminal after the crimes have been committed, of gathering up the wreckage of society after the devastation of an economic collapse, or of fighting a war that reason might have prevented, then government fails to satisfy those urgent human purposes, which, in essence, gave it its beginning and provide its present justification."[14] The President's statement draws a distinction between preventive and remedial measures, and argues for government's acting to forestall, through constructive economic and social measures, rather than always merely to repair the damage once it is done.

It was characteristic of the earlier liberalism that Senator William E. Borah, always an independent, denounced the proposed wages and hours bill as placing all the minimum-wage employees in the country under a board at Washington "over which they have no control and against which they can exercise no power. . . . I do not want to place the wage earners of this country under control of a bureau. . . . I am just as much opposed to bureaucracy as I am to dictatorship. I am not nearly so much concerned about dictatorship, which we ordinarily speak of, as I am about bureaucracy. . . . The most burdensome, the most demoralizing system of government on earth is the bureaucratic system of government."[15] Roosevelt's answer to that criticism would be that the securing of economic rights is a crucial requirement of the democratic political condition, and that this implies and requires that "the essential democracy of our Nation and the safety of our people depend not upon the absence of power, but upon lodging it with those whom the people can continue or change through an honest and free system of elections."[16] For it was the *absence* of power, or rather the unwillingness to exercise governmental power, as Roosevelt contended, that "brought us to the brink of disaster in 1932."[17] The broadening of the sphere of individual rights (that is, the establishment of fair and just conditions in the economic life of the nation) therefore required the enlargement of the functions of government which the New Deal proposed.

It is of particular importance to understand, moreover, that the New Dealers were experimenting with techniques of governmental control over concentrated economic power in contradistinction to the trust-busting solution of the earlier liberalism. When Senator Burton K. Wheeler, who had been La Follette's running mate in 1924, had led the fight in the Senate in 1935 for the passage of the public utility holding company control bill, he was careful to distinguish the piece of legislation he was sponsoring from the NRA, which he had opposed. The purpose of the holding company legislation, as he explained it, was to decentralize the few vast overconcentrated national organizations that controlled power plants over all the country. Wheeler believed that it was a necessary exercise of national political power to decentralize concentrated economic power; but the NRA, in his estimation, was an exercise of political power for the purpose of augmenting the economic power of organized industry.[18] FDR furnished a break with that tradition. The earlier liberalism and the New Dealers shared the view that the concentration of economic power constitutes a threat to democracy, but the earlier liberalism had similar fears about the concentration of governmental power. Accordingly, the earlier liberalism sought to decentralize concentrations of economic power, while the New Dealers were more inclined—with some exceptions, however—to use regulatory legislation to control such concentrations. The New Dealers, in contradistinction to the earlier liberalism, viewed a cooperation, not a conflict, between governmental power and private economic power, that is, between politics and private property, but with the political as the controlling element.

The earlier liberalism could be characterized as follows: the more fundamental issue of political reconstruction is almost entirely subordinated to the restoration of the old competitive system (i.e., improving private competiton or freedom of competition) that would require only a limited government. That liberalism called for the destruction of monopolies and trusts, not their regulation. There was the ill-defined recognition that some regulation was necessary and proper, but no principle was stated.[19] In the New Deal, on the other hand, there was a principle stated that the polity must undertake responsibility for the maintenance and health of the economy as a whole to the point of rearranging that economy, if necessary, and redistributing its benefits. This position moves away from an emphasis on the *conditions* of happiness toward the enjoyment or possession of happiness understood as material happiness or well-being. The welfare state is a society in which material happiness or well-being is no longer merely privately pursued. The question arises therefore as to whether one should understand this shift in emphasis as a qualitative shift in American politics as opposed, say, to a mere acceleration of political actions. This question, in turn, raises the further question of whether, if qualitative, the change in action was based upon a conscious change in political understanding.

Basil Rauch, a New Deal historian, asks whether the great series of New Deal measures, which included the National Labor Relations Act, the Social Security Act, and the Fair Labor Standards Act, represent a "new departure" in American political thought and practice. His answer is that "the sheer quantity of governmental reformist activity" initiated by the New Deal produced a "qualitative change" in American government —what is called positive government or the welfare state. Something new enters the tradition, Rauch admits, but it must be understood as derivative from the sheer quantity of reformist activity.[20] The quantitative change, from a certain moment on, becomes a qualitative change, and therefore the New Deal can be reduced to a series of legislative acts initiated by the Roosevelt administration. This interpretation of the New Deal leads to the consequence that there was no change, strictly speaking; that there was only a *fast* deal and *not* a new deal; and that all the fuss raised by the opposition was merely a reaction to the rapidity with which the series of New Deal legislative acts unfolded.

In Rauch, one sees reflections of the notion that the New Deal did unthinkingly what it was driven to do, and that the driving force was the boiling up of events and not the grasp of the significance of those events by FDR nor the direction given them by New Deal legislation. For to say that the qualitative change that had come about did so by the sheer force of the multiplicity of *ad hoc* responses to immediate problems is simply to say that the New Deal did not know what it was doing. The problem can be formulated as follows: did FDR lead or follow, and if he led, did he really know where he was going? Everyone agrees that he was not a theoretician, but a politician. What we do say is that Rauch reflects the prevalent view that practice makes theory and that we, on the other hand, believe that in the case of the New Deal in particular, as well as political events in general, it is the other way around. FDR did not know the deepest roots of, nor could he foresee, the fullest consequences of his political actions. But he did act, and he did know, *in principle*, the character of the change his actions were bringing about. Hence we may conclude that that principle was the directing force of the several legislative acts that made up the New Deal, no matter how clumsy or hasty some of those acts might have been.[21] It is no small evidence of this that FDR gave to the whole a name before any of its parts were cast; for he introduced the term "New Deal" in his acceptance speech for the presidential nomination in July, 1932: "I have . . . described the spirit of my program as a 'new deal,' which is plain English for a changed *concept* of the duty and responsibility of Government toward economic life."[22]

As we must repeat, the aim of the New Deal was the welfare state. To understand the welfare state means to understand it in its relation to a tradition. By viewing the welfare state in the light of the Lockean-Jeffersonian tradition, one can fairly see what Roosevelt's principles were. The Declaration of Independence defines the function of government in terms of a certain understanding of the relation between happiness and the conditions of happiness. According to that understanding, life, liberty and the pursuit of happiness constitute the conditions of happiness, and it is the function of government to guarantee those conditions, but not happiness itself. FDR, on the other hand, conceives the function of government to be to achieve the greater happiness of the greater number. He seems to see that happiness as well-being, and he defines his own understanding of the change in terms of the movement from political to economic rights. It is *this* fundamental change in emphasis that gives the New Deal its distinctive character as a political movement; for, from now on, government furnishes not only the conditions of happiness, but, to a considerable extent, the enjoyment or possession of material happiness which may properly be called *well-being*.[23] Well-being or welfare is a kind of in-between concept, in between the conditions of happiness and happiness itself. It seems clear, therefore, that Roosevelt, with a consideration of political principle in mind, tried to develop a thoughtful view of what the country ought to do in order to meet the crisis at hand. He was able, moreover, to articulate what was happening more successfully than any other man of that period.

The particular cause of the transition from traditional democracy to the welfare state, as we have tried to show, is the introduction of a new principle. But there is a sense in which that principle forms a part of the Hamiltonian viewpoint. The notion that the well-being or welfare of the greater number is to be provided for by government is implicit, although we cannot say it was explicitly recognized, in the Constitution's Preamble, which plainly declares that one of the great ends of government is to "promote the general welfare": ". . . in order to form a more perfect Union, establish justice, insure domestic tranquillity, provide for the common defense, promote the general welfare, and secure the blessings of liberty. . . . " It could reasonably be argued that the New Deal was in a real sense attempting to carry out that purpose announced in the Preamble; that is, the New Deal's intention of furthering the general welfare by governmental provision for material well-being could be construed as the pursuit of something stated in the Preamble, deflected perhaps by Roosevelt's turn of mind. That statement of purpose, moreover, is not limited to the Preamble, but is mentioned in the main body of the Constitution, in the clause granting the power to lay and collect taxes. The Social Security Act, called the cornerstone of the welfare side of the New Deal program, was based on the taxing power, and approved by the Supreme Court when that tribunal stated in 1937 that Congress may impose taxes to provide for the general welfare.[24] What Roosevelt did, and did in our opinion deliberately, was to develop more fully and express more deeply that purpose stated in the Preamble.

What we have suggested is that liberal democracy cannot reach clarity about itself if it does not possess a coherent and comprehensive understanding of its presuppositions and make intelligible the character of the *modifications* of its primary understanding of political things which have occurred throughout the course of American history. It suffices here to emphasize only that there was a sudden breakthrough in American political thought and practice in the 1930's which was accomplished by FDR and the New Deal. As a result of the climactic experience of the Great Depression, and the manner in which that depression was understood, the earlier liberalism became seriously threatened. What is of immense importance in understanding the politics of the New Deal period is that the controversy between FDR and the earlier liberalism was not constituted merely by the latter's reaction to the rapidity with which the series of New Deal legislative acts unfolded. It derived ultimately from different understandings of the intents and purposes of democratic society. The contribution the New Deal made to the American political tradition consisted of its correcting the earlier liberal view to the extent of correcting its narrowed understanding of the functions of government (or the relation between the government and the economy), and only in this light can we see the case for FDR and the New Deal in its full dimensions. Fundamental to the welfare-state position was Roosevelt's contention that "government has the final responsibility for the *well-being* of its citizenship," that is, for securing the material happiness or well-being of its citizens,[25] while the earlier liberalism, setting society apart from government, continued to believe in government as being necessary only under certain conditions. FDR believed that the ill-being of the greater number was the most serious threat to democratic government. Given the reality of that ill-being in the Great Depression, that was surely an ill to be cured.

Perhaps Roosevelt ought to have perceived that a preference for the well-being of the greater number does not add up to a comprehensive view of the good of society or the common good. On a somewhat higher level (although this would take us outside the Lockean frame of reference), government would be concerned with creating a certain moral tone and encouraging the development of human excellence. FDR never reached that point, however, for he did not conceive of the function of government as fostering the development of virtue or human excellence.[26] He considered the completion or perfection of the individual to be outside the framework of government as such, and was still guided by a rather limited view of happiness. But while the virtues of individualism as a substitute for human excellence continued to mean for Roosevelt what they meant for the tradition, he also knew that individualism was not enough. It was apparent to him that individual interests do not always operate in the public interest, and that unrestrained individualism has a natural tendency to turn individuals away from the public or common interest. He would subscribe to the view that the death of democracy occurs when individual interests or supposed individual interests become confused with real or common interests. Considered in this way, the continuous task of the democratic statesman would be to turn individuals in the direction of their common interests or the common good, that is, to establish the proper relationship between individual and common interests.

We hope we have shown how FDR's distinctive view of the common good points toward a more fundamental function for the government than that which was implicit in the earlier liberalism. But this change was not accomplished without very great difficulty because it involved a struggle against the established pattern of earlier liberal beliefs and attitudes. The essential failure of the earlier liberalism consisted in a one-sided and oversimplified concentration on individualism and all that this implies for politics and government. The correction of that view involves a realization that the function of government is more than a mere matter of guaranteeing life, liberty, and the pursuit of happiness, as has been so often supposed in our traditional political thinking. Surely Woodrow Wilson's New Freedom began to question the authority of the earlier liberalism. To the extent to which FDR has taught us that a democratic society requires for its preservation and improvement not merely the securing of political freedom on the lowest level but the guaranteeing of equality of opportunity through governmental provision for welfare or economic well-being, he transcends some of the limitations of liberal democracy and even enlarges its horizons. But FDR did not seem to realize that, in constantly seeking to strengthen economic equality, the human personality may in fact become submerged in the interest of a better-regulated economic life with its emphasis on health, welfare, and freedom from want. FDR may not have intended it that way, but the humane passion for welfarism could result in what Tocqueville referred to as a soft despotism. This is perhaps the greatest difficulty underlying the New Deal.

CHAPTER 10

Conclusion

AT some moments I thought Roosevelt saw how radical a reconstruction was called for; at others I guessed he would temporize as the transition was made. I was right in the last. The New Deal was a mild medicine.

Rexford G. Tugwell, 1960

In contrast to previous studies of Franklin D. Roosevelt, we have stressed the influence of the New Deal on American political thought. It surely would be unreasonable to claim that we have arrived at a comprehensive understanding of American democratic thought. The most we can hope to have achieved is to have partly pointed the way in studying that thought, or in studying certain critical aspects of that thought. Roosevelt's New Deal constituted a profound modification of the traditional American democracy, a modification arrived at through a break with the earlier liberalism. What that break effected by the New Deal means, one can see most clearly when one examines the great debates of that generation.

In studying the politics of the New Deal period, we used as points of departure the great controversies of that period—Roosevelt's struggle with the Supreme Court between 1935 and 1937, his attempted "purge" of Democratic congressmen in the 1938 party primaries, and the controversy over the third-term nomination in 1939 and 1940—which we have tried to analyze. One must always start with the massive and obvious. We have tried to understand these controversies as they revealed themselves on the surface; and then, in the process of abstracting from these events, we worked our way backward and deeper to the crucial question (or questions) underlying these controversies. And as it turns out, the question of a largely unregulated versus a regulated or controlled economy underlies the domestic political disputes of the 1930's (that is, the Supreme Court controversy and the "purge" and, to some extent, the third-term controversy).

In the light of the considerations set forth in the previous chapters (with the exception of the one on Yalta), we would not go too far in asserting that the most profound change the American democracy has hitherto undergone, the most important enlargement and deepening it has hitherto experienced, is due to Roosevelt and the New Deal. Even Richard Hofstadter admits this. There is no doubt that Roosevelt, considered as a thinker and a statesman, ranks lower than Abraham Lincoln. While one must admit that he proceeded with practical wisdom and moderation, one cannot compare him to Lincoln in terms of depth of understanding. The successful handling of the situation of the depression, that is, the preservation of liberal democratic institutions in a period of crisis, was one that involved an unusual degree of practical wisdom and moderation. Those qualities Roosevelt had, but that is not to say that he possessed theoretical wisdom.

The political potentialities of the presidential office have been brought out most clearly by Jefferson, Jackson, Lincoln, and Franklin Roosevelt. Roosevelt had a number of serious political setbacks in his White House career—the Supreme Court's invalidation of critical New Deal legislation in 1935 and 1936, the defeat of his "court-packing" plan in 1937, and his failure to remove recalcitrant Democratic congressmen in the 1938 party primaries. But the supreme test of the practicality of his politics was that none of these setbacks proved disastrous; for he was able to get the regulatory and welfare legislation he needed, change the complexion of the Supreme Court for the better, and prevent the Congress from blocking his interventionist foreign policy prior to the attack on Pearl Harbor. We do not know how Roosevelt himself would have characterized it, but we do know that his approach to the problems of the 1930's was intensely Hamiltonian. Roosevelt never forgot that government requires competence, energy, force, foresight, and something approaching wisdom. There was an emphasis in the New Deal on the positive function of government, a function that had been insufficiently acknowledged by the earlier liberalism. But it must be emphasized that, while the thrust of the New Deal points more clearly to Hamilton than to any other statesman, the New Deal is more than a mere restatement of Hamiltonianism. The objective of the New

Deal was the welfare state, and the coming into being of the welfare state required the emergence of a higher plane of thought regarding the American ends than that which informed the Progressive Movement. That higher plane restored the vigorous view of active government which the Founding Fathers themselves had and restored the proper relation between the purposes of the Preamble and the body of the Constitution. Surely the New Deal pointed in the direction of the restoration of the highest aims of the Constitution. If it can be said that the New Deal *changed* the Constitution, or went beyond it, our argument is that it did so in the direction toward which the Constitution itself pointed.

The question arises as to whether the changes effected by the New Deal (that is, the coming into being of the welfare state), should be understood as a regime change or as a continuation of the existing regime. If there is any lesson to be learned from studying Roosevelt's statesmanship, it is that of seeing how the American democracy could be improved *without* being fundamentally changed. The great task for Roosevelt was that of re-creating democratic political institutions, which was tantamount to the introduction of a new quality into the regime. But the introduction of that new quality was done in such a way as to preserve the essential nature of the regime, that is, its democratic nature. We may go so far as to regard the establishment of the welfare state as the most important event in American history in the twentieth century. The establishment of the welfare state is the most profound modification of the traditional liberalism that has occurred, but it is not the end of liberalism.

Needless to say, from this point of view, we had to consider that change in orientation which found its expression in the welfare state. It is of some importance for an understanding of the welfare state to realize that it is a relatively recent phenomenon in American politics. Therefore the welfare state presupposes somewhere and somehow a change in the earlier practice, and all changes of any importance constitute a break with the earlier practice. It seems that the accepted interpretations of the New Deal do not pay sufficient attention to the distinctive character of its innovations; furthermore, the accepted interpretations are based on what amounts to a depreciation of the welfare state as a departure from the earlier liberalism. Owing to the collapse of the earlier liberalism, it became necessary to reexamine liberalism as such with a view to the question of whether the traditional understanding of the relationship between the government and the economy was adequate. The central errors of the earlier liberalism, Roosevelt maintained, were its unrestricted individualism, its policy of encouraging smallness and discouraging economic concentration (that is, its antitrust approach of breaking down and destroying concentrated economic power), and its narrow and inflexible view of the functions of government. The Great Depression had thrust upon the government the responsibility for the general performance of the economy. FDR's New Deal rejected the notion that an economic system such as that of the United States would regulate itself automatically by the uncontrolled competition of private enterprise, and therefore it imposed regulations and controls on the economy as a whole. That rejection, moreover, was predicated on a certain way of looking at the relationship between welfare or economic well-being and government (that is, that welfare or well-being is a vitally desirable function of government).

The specific New Deal thesis was that government has the responsibility to provide not merely for the conditions of happiness (i.e., the Lockeanism implicit in the American Founding) but for something approaching happiness itself or what we may call well-being or welfare. The difference between the welfare state and the Lockean-Jeffersonian liberalism would then seem to be rooted in the fundamental difference between happiness or well-being and the pursuit of happiness as the aim or end of the state. Locke surely had much to do with the American Founding, but that Lockeanism is not identical with the regime as reinterpreted by the New Deal.

Roosevelt's New Deal has been described by some as "the prologue to Communism in America";[1] and, in order to substantiate that view, his critics have emphasized that he was fomenting class war by using the rhetoric of the class struggle against the great industrial and financial interests. As a matter of fact, his rhetoric clearly exaggerated the existing state of the danger, at least from them, but his intention was to expose the threat to capitalism from the capitalists themselves by exaggerating it. It seems to be clear that Roosevelt recognized and generally exercised moderation. That he wanted at the same time to appeal to popular prejudice is not at all surprising considering the resistance of powerful moneyed interests to his programs and policies. The way in which he did this indicates, however, that he sometimes departed from a course of moderation. But there is no suggestion here that Roosevelt ever intended to undermine American democracy. Roosevelt's first inaugural address is one of the great presidential inaugural speeches in American history, clearly ranking with those of Thomas Jefferson and Abraham Lincoln. If that speech is indicative of anything at all, it shows how deeply he was steeped in the American democratic tradition and in the rhetoric of that tradition. We find ourselves prepared for this fact by the realization that the New Deal does not emerge through the rejection or annihilation of the tradition but through its reshaping or reinterpretation.

We have indicated our reasons for believing that FDR's New Deal was not a mere extension of the earlier liberalism or progressivism. The consciousness of the critics of FDR, from both the left and the right, has been so dominated by the notion that he was a "pragmatic" politician that they have failed to recognize the character of his distinctive contribution to American political thought. Roosevelt added a new dimension to American political practice and surely to American political thought (which stands behind the practice); for in the tension between progressivism and socialism, he, and through him, the country, rose above those alternatives. As Adolph A. Berle, Jr., that member of the original Brains Trust who was closest to Roosevelt's own thinking, recently wrote:

> We certainly refused to take advantage of the economic collapse to set up state socialism (let alone Communism) or to intrigue within the government to prepare such a development. We did undertake through democratically adopted measures to redistribute the national income, steering more of it toward the least favored among the population. We hoped for a better distribution of wealth. We did intend that the federal government should take over the ultimate controls of currency and credit (as it did), and the power, where necessary, to allocate capital resources as well, . . . while maintaining non-statist enterprise as the major method of production.[2]

The New Deal therefore may be properly described as a reforming rather than a revolutionary movement.

APPENDIX 1

Political Philosophy and The American Political Tradition

THE purpose of this essay is to discuss the continuing relevance of Richard Hofstadter's book *The American Political Tradition*, a series of essays analyzing the postures of American political leaders, for those essays have had a profound influence on the study of American political thought. The book is of special importance, not only because of the tradition against which it is directed, but also because it systematically underrates the importance of American statesmanship and, by indirection, the quality of the political teaching implicit in that statesmanship. Hofstadter teaches that the American political tradition is a fundamentally debased democratic tradition. Ultimately, the criticism he levels against the tradition is a criticism leveled against politics or against a tradition inordinately in love with politics, the Lockean tradition. But he never suggests the conditions that must be fulfilled for a transformation of the tradition. He therefore offers no solution to the tradition's debasement as a democratic tradition.

The book is certainly a challenge to the American political tradition (unlike Louis Hartz's *The Liberal Tradition in America* and Daniel J. Boorstin's *The Genius of American Politics*), but that challenge is presented with such caution and circumspection that it hardly appears as a challenge at all. In considering the problem posed by the tradition's political debasement, Hofstadter says: "Although it has been said repeatedly that we need *a new conception of the world* to replace the ideology of self-help, free enterprise, competition, and beneficent cupidity upon which Americans have been nourished since the foundation of the Republic, no new conceptions of comparable strength have taken root and no statesman with a great mass following has arisen to propound them."[1] But one must attend with utmost care to the manner of his analysis, for he does not say what that new conception of the world should be like. He never presents an alternative, at least not explicitly, though we may perhaps infer it from the distinction he brings to our attention between a democracy of cupidity and a democracy of fraternity.[2]

In explaining his intention to his readers, Hofstadter says: "In a corporate and consolidated society demanding international responsibility, cohesion, centralization, and planning, the traditional ground is shifting under our feet. It is *imperative* in a time of cultural crisis to gain fresh perspectives on the past."[3] He says little more than that here, other than referring to the need for "a reinterpretation of our political traditions."[4] Hofstadter demands that the present generation reinterpret the American traditions on the basis of its own experiences and with a view to its own future (and presumably this would apply also to his own reinterpretation). His reinterpretation therefore has a futuristic character; that is, it is guided by considerations of an anticipated or desirable future. Yet fundamental to that reinterpretation or critical understanding is his distinction between a democracy of cupidity and a democracy of fraternity, and in the discussion of the postures of American statesmen which follows, there is a constant interplay between these alternative conceptions of democracy.

The first requirement for critically understanding and analyzing our political traditions would be to have alternative democratic regimes available. The different kinds of democracy vary as the principle of democracy is variously combined with other principles. The massive fact about the American political traditions, as Hofstadter sees them, is that they are concerned almost exclusively with individual self-interest and are driven by unlimited selfishness or cupidity. Clearly cupidity or covetousness of wealth is a destructive principle and cannot therefore be fully consistent with Hofstadter's understanding of the democratic principle. More specifically, a democracy of cupidity (which he says the American democracy is) is a defective democratic regime because of the defects in the system of private property. The indefeasible roots of private property are self-interest and self-assertion.

Hofstadter's criticism of the American political tradition necessarily implies a difference between things as they are and things as they ought to be, and the standard by which that difference can be understood is humanism. It is certainly true that the political teaching that underlies this book is humanistic, and Hofstadter's humanism is inseparable from the way in which he understands democracy. The humane democracy he favors is a democracy of fraternity which looks beyond the divisiveness of propertied selfishness to the fraternity of mankind.[5] His animus against individualism and competitiveness can be best understood in terms of a changed attitude toward property and, more particularly, in terms of a belief in the divisiveness of property.

Hofstadter calls our attention to the fact that the major political traditions in America have shared a belief in the economic values of a capitalist culture, that is, in the rights of property, the philosophy of economic individualism, and the value of competition. He points out that this tradition is democratic because it follows the egalitarian principle, but it is a democracy of cupidity rather than a democracy of fraternity.[6] It is necessary to explain briefly what Hofstadter understands by a democracy of fraternity. Fraternity strictly understood means that all men are brothers. A political society, in order to be a good political society, must be inspired by fraternity, which (as we know from the Rousseauean analysis) is compounded of equality and compassion. Hofstadter envisions the fraternity of mankind and regards property as the chief dissolver of the natural bond of affection and sympathy which joins mankind as a species.[7] He seems to suggest that a fraternal sense of community can be approached through a radical correction of the property relation. We can leave it at these general remarks for the present.

Some of the assumptions underlying Hofstadter's book are indicated in his chapter on the Founding Fathers. The Founding Fathers, he says, thought that man was a creature of rapacious self-interest, and yet they wanted him to be free to contend, to engage in an umpired strife, to use property to get property. But in an ingenious way, he suggests, that very self-interest was exploited to the end of reconciling self-interest and freedom. Self-interest, when correctly managed, can secure freedom, propertied freedom, which means freedom for the owners of property. Accordingly, they constructed a framework of "balanced government," a harmonious system of mutual frustration, with ample constitutional devices that would force various interests to check and control one another in the interest of that freedom. In their minds, says Hofstadter, freedom was linked, not to democracy, but to property.[8] He regards the work of the Founding Fathers as deficient in this decisive respect. A transformation of the tradition the Founders set in motion would mean transforming the corrupt, predominantly Hobbesian-Lockean society, which is in a state of constant competition, interest with interest, faction with faction, into an order based on new and different principles.

Hofstadter's discussion of the Founding Fathers culminates in the assertion that modern humanistic thinkers who seek for a means by which society may transcend eternal conflict and rigid adherence to property rights as its integrating principles can expect *no answer* in the philosophy of balanced government as it was set down by the Constitution makers.[9] It seems as if Hofstadter is animated by the certainty that the future will bring about the realization of certain possibilities, whereas the Founding Fathers did not live in such an open horizon, but in a horizon closed by the possibilities known at that time. Hofstadter teaches that the thought of the Founding Fathers is essentially related to the eighteenth century, and that therefore it cannot reasonably claim to be valid beyond the historical situation to which it is related.

Virtually all the chapters in this book are devoted to a discussion of practical politicians. The only chapter not devoted as a whole to a practical politician or politicians is devoted to an abolitionist orator—Wendell Phillips—who represented the priceless provincial *integrity* that could be found in mid-century America wherever the seeds of Puritanism had been sown. Phillips's conduct not even remotely reminds us of that of a practical politician, let alone a major party figure or holder of high political office; he is simply an agitator with an ax to grind. His role as an agitator, which distinguishes him from all other practical men treated, makes him, according to Hofstadter, a man of transcendent moral principle whose function is to influence the public mind in the interest of some large social transformation, namely, abolitionism.[10] Hofstadter seems to allow that political success requires something more than principle; for he says that abolitionism, as it became more dilute in principle, somehow became stronger as an actual menace to slavery. But he explains its success only in terms of its becoming linked with a "strategy qualified by opportunism," that is, in terms of abolitionism using a major political party as a vehicle and therefore linking the antislavery issue with other, more material, issues.[11] Hofstadter believes that any political action that requires a dilution in principle is opportunistic, in this case, abolitionism taking its place within the compromising framework of an overall party program and hence abandoning its theoretical purity. This notion, however, fails to recognize that prudence or practical wisdom is precisely an adaptation of principle to circumstance. Perhaps it is more a consideration of circumstance than of principle. But that does not mean that prudence is opportunism; it is rather the very difficult task of meeting, in the light of principle, the particular requirements of circumstance.

It comes as no surprise to learn that Hofstadter describes FDR as one who practices opportunism in politics. Opportunism is ordinarily understood as a policy of doing what is at the time expedient, as opposed to rigid adherence to principle; it is meant to imply sacrifice of principle or an undue spirit of accommodation to present circumstance. And with a view to the fact that opportunism is the opposite of principle, the development of Roosevelt's more important reform measures is explained by Hofstadter as the result of a strategy of accommodation rather than as a matter of conviction.[12] For example, he argues that Roosevelt was never terribly enthusiastic about labor relations legislation and that his eventual support of the NLRA was not based on any real commitment. Hofstadter treats Roosevelt as an opportunist; indeed, he implies that none of the actions credited to him are really to be taken that seriously. At the same time, however, his criticism seems to lose some of its force upon closer examination. Thanks to Roosevelt's initiative, Hofstadter admits, the keel of economic life in America had been righted and politics turned safely back on its normal course.[13] But Hofstadter has not reflected on the possibility that, if that consideration is to be taken seriously, then perhaps much more is also to be taken seriously. The difficulty with his position is revealed by the fact that Roosevelt's political successes (that he demonstrated the viability of liberal democratic institutions at a most critical time in the nation's history) would be hard to understand in terms of mere opportunism.

Hofstadter's deficient characterization of FDR reveals a fault in his serious argument, for the particular wisdom conveyed through statesmen or politicians cannot be understood adequately except with a view to the distinction between opportunism and prudence. The question is whether FDR was an opportunist or not. I am convinced that he was not, surely not in the sense in which Hofstadter means it. He was not careless of principle. He sought to preserve or reconstruct a government, not incidentally or merely as a way of keeping himself in political office, but as a part of his principles. But to make principles meaningful, as Roosevelt surely understood, one must consider the manner in which they are implemented. Hofstadter's emphasis on Roosevelt as an opportunist (as conveyed through the title and the argument of that chapter) is misleading to the extent that it directs our attention away from the necessary circumstances that must be taken into account if politics is to be taken seriously. As his discussion of Wendell Phillips shows, Hofstadter is well aware that principle is not the only thing necessary for success in politics. He himself admits that there are circumstances in which principle would need to be qualified by something else in order to have any practical consequences. It is inevitably necessary to apply principle to variable circumstances; but in any circumstances there is, properly speaking, some dilution of principle and that dilution is called prudence. But Hofstadter denies the decisive importance of finding the right dilution of principle that best suits the specific circumstances at a given time by calling any dilution in principle "opportunism."

In the perspective in which Hofstadter discusses the problem of the American tradition, as we have already seen, the distinction between opportunism and prudence tends to disappear. The difficulty to which his criticism is exposed is concentrated in his attempt to replace prudence by opportunism, which shows how far he is from understanding the essential function of the statesman. Surely actions prompted by prudence are fundamentally different from actions prompted by opportunism, and the difference between them would appear to be rooted in the difference of motive or intent. The motive or intent of FDR's statesmenship during the period of the depression was to show how the American democracy could be *improved* without being fundamentally *changed*. Hofstadter says that, although FDR's argument carried to the brink of socialism, it was not socialism that he was proposing.[14] It is fairly clear that Hofstadter would have changed what FDR preserved. Hofstadter, indeed many warm partisans of FDR, did not really know that he was attempting to preserve something; therefore, what appeared to them as a failure on his part may really have been a great success. He failed to achieve what they would have aimed at; but, since that was not his aim, he did not in fact fail.

Hofstadter identifies his book as a history of political thinking, and, as such, we may expect to learn something from it about the problem of the American political tradition and the relation of that problem to political philosophy proper.[15] The book is therefore not without a theoretical perspective. That theoretical perspective, however, is limited, and the book as a whole is inadequate as a criticism of the American tradition. Hofstadter decides without hesitation in favor of a clearly articulated break with the tradition, for he wants to transform the tradition into something other than what it is. The whole book is a suggestion for the transformation of the American political tradition; hence the decisive action of the book is one of transformation or change. But he preaches change without thinking through the terms of that change. Very much, not to say everything, would seem to depend on his assertion that the American tradition is a tradition characterized *simply* by the ideology of self-help, free enterprise, competition, and beneficent cupidity.

Hofstadter has put together a marvelous abstraction that reveals the nature of everything he sees by taking the shape of that abstraction. He argues that the pervasive quality of American politics (that is, the emphasis on propertied selfishness) can be traced to the requirement of enlightened self-interest or selfishness in its Lockean formulation. But the view conveyed by the book as a whole exhibits the lowest common denominator of the tradition without showing what has been grafted onto that base of enlightened selfishness he makes so much of. In his analysis of Abraham Lincoln's political thought, Professor Harry Jaffa has suggested what Lincoln has added to the tradition above and beyond what the Founding Fathers said and understood. As we can learn from reading Jaffa, whereas in the Lockean perspective the benefiting of others is ultimately reduced to self-interest, in Lincoln's subtle reinterpretation self-interest and well-doing ultimately coincide, inasmuch as the greatest self-satisfaction is conceived as service to others.[16] But what Hofstadter sees is only the

Lockean origins of the tradition. He does not see that Lincoln's perspective, which forms a very important part of that tradition, transcends the Lockeanism of the founders of the tradition (without abandoning the lower-level Lockean demands).

Hofstadter draws our attention to the movement of thought that underlies the tradition by attempting to show how individuals are encouraged or compelled to think only of their immediate self-interest, not of the common good. He emphasizes, therefore, that the American tradition can only be understood from a philosophic perspective like that of Hobbes, and, by implication, that of Locke.[17] The difficulty with this interpretation is that it reveals an oversimplified understanding of the relationship between political philosophy (in this case Lockeanism) and the American political tradition. That relationship is misstated by Hofstadter; for, by placing Lockeanism at the core of his criticism, he exhibits only the most common, the lowest, ingredient of the tradition. His emphasis on the overwhelming importance of the tradition's Lockean roots has tended to neglect those added ingredients that have been grafted onto that tradition and that have altered that tradition to some extent. The mere change from property to pursuit of happiness in the Declaration of Independence itself shows that we are reading Thomas Jefferson and not pure Locke. To be sure, it can be readily shown that the Declaration presupposes Lockean political philosophy and is based largely on it. But the third natural right in Locke is property, and in the Declaration, it is not property but the pursuit of happiness. That's a very important difference which Hofstadter has never considered. One would have to see what the understanding of Jefferson (not to mention Lincoln and others) has added to the understanding of Locke, and how that understanding became incorporated into the tradition, in order to clarify the relationship between theory and practice.

The American Political Tradition poses a problem of great theoretical significance for students of American political thought. It is not always recognized that political philosophy has been the moving force in the American political tradition only primarily through the intermediation of its statesmen (including of course its jurists or judicial statesmen). To see how this articulation between political philosophy and the American political tradition has actually worked, one would have to study what American statesmen have thought about what they had done or were planning to do. This point needs to be stressed because Hofstadter is unable to recognize statesmanship in politics. He limits the meaning of politics to strategies employed to maximize interest or influence or to compromise competing interests and influences (despite his occasional tributes to an Alexander Hamilton or a Franklin D. Roosevelt). Hence he could not take that tradition seriously, for to take it seriously would mean to regard it as possible that the men who made and continued the tradition were serious-minded in dealing with the fundamental problems of politics. Hofstadter discounted parts of his book, to some extent, ten years after its initial publication. He said, on that later occasion, that his opinion of FDR as a politician had gone up as his understanding of what can and cannot be done in the political processes had increased.[18] We have no reason to doubt that he meant what he said in this regard. Although these kinds of corrections tend to weaken the certainty of his overall criticism, the book still remains his broadest statement of the problem of the American political tradition.

The argument of his book is simple and can be stated in a very few words. Hofstadter presents or interprets the American political tradition; and, as a democratic tradition, he finds it wanting. As a matter of principle, he prefers the more democratic democracy of fraternity to the less democratic democracy of cupidity. From this it follows that the criterion he uses for distinguishing between alternative democratic regimes is fraternity, which is compounded of equality and compassion. But while Hofstadter says that the critical issue for the American democracy is that of developing a new conception of the world to replace the ideology of enlightened self-interest, he never sets forth what he means by a democracy of fraternity. The clearest indication of this is that the term *Humanism* is only alluded to and is not in any way developed. To that extent, the book rests on presuppositions that are never clarified; for to have criticisms of the tradition in the name of humanism means merely, in Hofstadter's case, to have criticisms without feeling compelled to indicate the way of life for the sake of which the criticisms are made.

Hofstadter, moreover, in analyzing the postures of American political leaders, does not pay sufficient attention to the harsh political circumstances which necessarily impose obstacles on even the most desirable reforms. He fails to appreciate the fact that a statesman has only a limited control over the circumstances within which he must act. In more general terms, what does this all mean? The consequence is an enormous oversimplification of the political issues involved and, above all, it tends to downgrade deliberation and judgment. The attempt to substitute opportunism for prudence tends to narrow or eliminate the possibilities for deliberation and judgment as relevant factors in the political process. Hofstadter's doctrinairism leaves no room for prudence in the course of his analysis of the postures of American political leaders. Hofstadter rejects the politics of compromise, the politics of prudence. He sees only opportunism because that's all he wants to see.

The criticism of the American political tradition in Hofstadter is inseparable from a criticism of politics in general (and it is against this very orientation that our criticism is directed). Hofstadter says that the processes of politics normally involve exaggeration, myth making, and fierce animosities.[19] But it soon becomes clear that this basic understanding is meant to apply also to the most serious political controversies in American history. The political process is the process by which we deal with our political problems, the problems of conservation and reform. it demands, although it does not always get, deliberation and judgment and measure. But according to Hofstadter, the fundamental fact of the political process is myth making. He sees no distinction whatsoever between myth making on the one hand and measured speech and action on the other. All of Hofstadter's difficulties could be said to arise out of this failure to rise to the level of precise distinctions.

Starting from the distinction between a democracy of cupidity and a democracy of fraternity, already noted, Hofstadter asserts that calculation and self-interest are not strong enough as social bonds and that friendship is required for the well-being of a democratic society. But as critical students of political science, we must ask ourselves whether a fraternal community would in fact be a free society. It seems to us that there is a very great danger involved in turning a vast nation loose in its sentimentality, even loose in the generous sentimentality of compassion or fraternity. And I think that one can see the handwriting on the wall if one looks at Lenin's *State and Revolution* in his discussion of the self-acting armed organization of the population.[20] What Hofstadter perhaps does not understand at all is that one cannot have a democracy of fraternity in an enormous country. Therefore, whatever difficulties may exist in Locke, one must not overlook the fact that any attempt to go beyond Locke must take into account that the Lockean regime is structurally more attuned to the questions of practicality. One of the beauties of Lockean theory, as most thoughtful liberals and conservatives would admit, is that it aims for a regime to be drafted in terms of constitutions and laws and the measured separation of powers. That theory recognizes, moreover, that prudential statesmen will not always be at the helm, and therefore it establishes a regime that will somehow weather the storm. The incongruous thing about Hofstadter is that he would abandon the limitations inherent in a Lockean regime in favor of a fraternal community without even recognizing the necessity there for an even greater measure of prudence than that which is required by the limited democracy of the United States.

APPENDIX 2

The Place of Theory in American Political Life

EDMUND Burke described the theory contained in his *An Appeal from the New to the Old Whigs* as intended to illustrate the principles of a constitution "already made," but not to furnish principles for making a "new" constitution: "It is a theory drawn from the *fact* of our government."[1] The neo-Burkeanism of Daniel J. Boorstin's influential book, entitled *The Genius of American Politics*, is apparent.[2] The thesis of this book can be described in the following terms: the one sure symptom of an ill-conducted state is the propensity of the people to resort to theories or blueprints. The characteristic tyrannies of our time—nazism, fascism, and communism—have expressed precisely this fascination for blueprints. And this is understood by Boorstin as the attempt "to replace history by philosophy." The "genius of American politics" resides in the fact that we have fashioned a "new" society *without* a blueprint. Americans are traditionally ill-qualified to build a democratic political theory, says Boorstin, and are the better off for it.

There is a preliminary discussion in which Boorstin opposes the "historical" notion of Burke to the use of the philosophies of Rousseau and Marx as blueprints for making constitutions. What Rousseau and the French Revolution and the Marxists did was to make constitutions or plan regimes, and that was bad. The only way to have a good constitution is to have one that has grown. A "made" constitution means something artificial and a "grown" constitution means something natural. The Rousseauean or Marxian emphasis on plan or design is rejected because that would be detrimental to freedom. Still, Boorstin has to face the fact that his favorite constitution—the American Constitution—is *not* a grown constitution but one that was made at a particular time in a convention. But he would say that the American Constitution was only the old English Constitution with certain modifications. And that the best evidence of this borrowing is the value we still attach to "our inheritance" from the English Constitution.[3]

In his chapter on the American Revolution, Boorstin is critical of certain historians who tends"to emphasize—or rather exaggerate—the similarity of ours to all other modern revolutions." Hence those historians have exaggerated the significance of what is supposed to have been the "ideology" of our Revolution.[4] And this exaggeration, Boorstin explains, is based on the idea that political controversy has a natural and inevitable tendency to express itself in universal terms.[5] Over against this view, he asserts that the American Revolution was hardly a revolution at all. It was something entirely different from that new kind of revolution the French had accomplished, for here there was "no long-drawn-out agitation, no intellectual war of attrition, of the sort that breeds dogmas and intransigence."[6] Boorstin adopts the view that the American revolt against English rule took place in the name of the traditional rights of English subjects which George III had sworn to uphold but had not.[7] And natural rights were not really an issue. As he indicates, the first important republican tract issued in America, Tom Paine's *Common Sense*, did not appear until six months after the Declaration of Independence, thus revealing the poverty of our political theorizing in the revolutionary period.[8]

The "liberal" historians come under Boorstin's criticism for their unwillingness to believe that the men of the Revolution meant exactly what they said: "[In] this age of Marx and Freud we have begun to take it for granted that, if people talk about one thing, they must be thinking about something else." And he continues: "... men like Jefferson and Adams all along meant what they were saying, that is, that the Revolution had something to do with the British Constitution."[9] But it should be mentioned here that the issue of natural rights was immensely appealing to Americans in 1776, and that Hamilton had written in 1775 that "the sacred rights of mankind are not to be rummaged for among old parchments or musty records. They are written as with a sunbeam, in the whole volume of human nature, by the hand of the divinity itself; and can never be erased or obscured by mortal power."[10]

Boorstin uses Tocqueville's description of the French Revolution as an example of what the American Revolution was not; that is, the French Revolution was one that concerned itself with the rights of man. But Paine, who was involved in both revolutions, saw a radical difference between the American and French revolutions on the one hand, and all earlier revolutions on the other. The earlier revolutions, as Paine explained, "had nothing in them that interested the bulk of mankind. They extended only to a change of persons and measures, but not of principles, and rose and fell among the common transactions of the moment." But, Paine continues, "within the space of a few years we have seen two revolutions, those of America and France. . . . From both these instances it is evident that the greatest force that can be brought into the field of revolutions are reason and common interest." And this, in Paine's understanding, is obviously something entirely different from the old kind of revolutions that had nothing in them that could influence beyond the spot that produced them.[11] Whatever might be said about the "conservative" character of the American Revolution, it cannot even be considered before one has fully realized that not all the men of the Revolution—Hamilton and Paine being cases in point—understood their revolution simply in the terms outlined by Boorstin.

We have repeated the equality proposition in the Declaration of Independence, says Boorstin, without bothering to discover what it originally meant and without realizing that probably none of the men who spoke it at the time meant by it what we would like it to mean.[12] We would like it to mean (I presume this is what Boorstin implies) the inclusion of all men regardless of color or other differentiating features. But Boorstin appears convinced that the equality proposition was *not* meant to include the Black American as far as eighteenth-century America was concerned. And he reminds us that the "life, liberty and pursuit of happiness" part of the Declaration was "two-thirds borrowed."[13] Indeed, all the prominent public men of the Revolution read the more general part of the Declaration as a borrowing of the sentiments contained in Locke's *Second Treatise of Government*. In that treatise, Locke speaks of man in a state of equality, and he seeks to prove that equality by man's being a member of a single species.[14] And granted that all men are equal, freedom is derivative from that equality, that is, if all men are equal, no man is governor over another man, and hence all men are free. This is the same order, equality first, and then freedom, that is found in the Declaration. The view of the Declaration is clearly Locke's view, with the primary stress being placed on the equality of all men, and freedom following from that equality. Boorstin's understanding of the more general part of the Declaration (that it was not whole-heartedly a statement of the universality of the equality proposition) is inconsistent with its known philosophic antecedent, Locke's *Second Treatise.* Therefore we would suggest that he fails to consider properly the connection between the Declaration and the political theory to which it is linked.

Chief Justice Taney had argued in the Dred Scott decision that the authors of the Declaration had not intended to include the Negro in their equality proposition, and Boorstin considers the Taney thesis historically "convincing."[15] In that decision, Taney cites a Massachusetts law of 1705 and a Maryland law of 1717 discriminating against Negroes as a "faithful index" of the state of feeling in the British colonies throughout the entire eighteenth century. And he tries to reconcile that state of feeling with the language of the Declaration by denying that the phrase "all men" was really meant to include the Black American. He observed that the conduct of those who framed the Declaration (that is, the fact that some of them were slaveholders) would have been inconsistent with the principles they asserted if they had meant to include the Black American in the equality proposition.[16] But Justice Curtis's dissent in that same case reveals that "at the time of the ratification of the Articles of Confederation, all free native-born inhabitants of New Hampshire, Massachusetts, New York, New Jersey, and North Carolina, though descended from African slaves, were not only citizens of those States, but such of them as had the other necessary qualifications possessed the franchise of electors, on equal terms with other citizens." Therefore, Curtis opposed the historical inaccuracy of the Taney statements.[17] The question of whether the Declaration was, or was not, a statement of universal political rights, as Lincoln explained, turns on the distinction between the *possession* and *enjoyment* of inalienable natural rights. In his speech on the Dred Scott decision, Lincoln stated that the authors of the Declaration defined

with tolerable distinctness, in what respects they did consider all men created equal—equal in "certain inalienable rights, among which are life, liberty and the pursuit of happiness." ... They did not mean to assert the obvious untruth, that all men were then actually enjoying that equality, nor yet, that they were about to confer it immediately upon them.... They meant to set up a standard maxim for a free society, which could be familiar to all, and revered by all; constantly looked to, constantly labored for, and even spreading and deepening its influence, and augmenting the happiness and value of life to all people of all colors everywhere.[18]

Taney fails to recognize that a right may be possessed without actually being enjoyed. In fact, this is what distinguished a *natural* right from a *positive* right in the eighteenth-century mind. Taney does not distinguish between natural and positive right, although it is unambiguously stated in the Declaration that the rights of man are derivative from "the laws of Nature and Nature's God"; that is, the equality proposition is clearly presented as a statement of *natural* right.[19]

Boorstin says that the Declaration was directed to the "opinions" and not to the "regeneration" of mankind.[20] And precisely because it was directed to the opinions of mankind, and not merely to the opinions of Englishmen, or those subject to English law, it attempted to justify that appeal in terms of "the laws of Nature and Nature's God" rather than in terms of the laws of England. But the full force of its appeal consisted in the expectation that sooner or later mankind would be capable of regenerating itself along the very lines stated in the Declaration. As Lincoln observed in a speech in reply to Senator Douglas in 1858: " 'We hold these truths to be self-evident, that all men are created equal' ... [This principle] is the electric cord in that Declaration that links the hearts of patriotic and liberty-loving men together, that will link those patriotic hearts as long as the love of freedom exists in the minds of men throughout the world."[21] Indeed, the particular principles stated in the Declaration were understood as universal principles that were sooner or later capable of being actualized everywhere, that is, of regenerating mankind.[22]

Jefferson had been widely considered the leading political theorist of the American Revolution, says Boorstin, but in reality it was Edmund Burke, who was also "the great theorist of British conservatism."[23] Surely Burke's incisive criticism of British doctrinairism during the period of the American Revolution deserves our everlasting gratitude. But still he can never replace the author of the Declaration of Independence as the leading political theorist of the American Revolution. It was not Edmund Burke but Thomas Jefferson who, as Abraham Lincoln so beautifully described it, had "the coolness, forecast, and capacity to introduce into a merely revolutionary document, an abstract truth, applicable to all men and all times, and so to embalm it there, that to-day, and in all coming days, it shall be a rebuke and a stumbling-block to the very harbingers of re-appearing tyranny and oppression."[24] Boorstin describes the American Revolution as "a prudential decision taken by men of principle rather than the affirmation of a theory," but he never states what those "principles" were to which the statesmen of the founding generation adhered.[25] And that failure follows, we would assert, from his denial of the natural-rights character of our Revolution.

Boorstin also contends that *The Federalist Papers* were "conspicuously lacking in a theory. . . . They had a simple practical purpose: to persuade the people of the state of New York to ratify the recently drawn federal Constitution."[26] And he distinguishes these papers from the writings of Locke and other political theorists, "which gave us either systematic theories of the state or wide-ranging speculation."[27] We would say that, with a small number of exceptions, all writings are written for the times. In fact, Locke himself, whose intentions are contrasted with those of *The Federalist Papers,* indicates in his Preface to the *Two Treatises* that he intends them as pamphlets supporting the Act of Settlement of 1688. As Locke states: "These [papers], I hope are sufficient to establish the Throne of our Great Restorer, Our present King William; to make good his Title, in the Consent of the People, which, being the only one of all lawful Governments, he had more fully and clearly than any Prince in Christendom: And to justify to the world the People of England, whose love of their Just and Natural Rights, with their resolution to preserve them, saved the Nation when it was on the very brink of Slavery and Ruine." In this respect, the *Treatises* were written for the times; but still Locke is important for his appeal to a universal principle concerning liberty and equality and government by consent, and in that sense the *Treatises* point beyond their times. In other words, the *Treatises* and *The Federalist Papers* have a good deal more in common than Boorstin would be willing to admit: the hard and fast distinction between pamphleteering and political theorizing is not at all clear in the political writings of Locke.

Boorstin reproduces a passage from Montesquieu on the necessity for a republican government,[28] an argument that had been borrowed in the "antifederalist" writings and that Hamilton countered in the ninth *Federalist* and Madison in other numbers. Simply stated, the "antifederalists" rested their argument on a theoretical view, and in order to combat that view the authors of *The Federalist Papers* addressed themselves to the question of whether a sound republican order could exist on a more extended basis than a state. As Boorstin himself confesses: "One of the main questions which disturbed people at the time of the foundation of the federal Union was whether a republican government can long endure, or even exist, over an extensive and varied continent."[29] And if the new Constitution were to be adopted, convincing proof of its merits would have to be placed before the citizens of the states. That convincing proof consisted partly in demonstrating "the utility of the Union," but above and beyond that in elaborating the basis upon which a sound republican order could be constructed, and that elaboration is what makes these papers treatiselike in character. We must underscore Boorstin's statement that "the organization of *The Federalist* papers . . . proceed[s] from the actual dangers which confronted Americans to the weakness of the existing confederation and the specific advantages of the various provisions of the new constitution."[30] But what he does not take into account is that the most important section of the papers contains a theoretical argument directed against the "antifederalist" thesis that republicanism cannot exist on an extended basis. Indeed, these papers are not conspicuously lacking in a theory. The Articles of Confederation was not a republican government but a republican confederation or a confederation of republics. And the new Constitution achieved a republican solution to the problems inherent in confederations, and in our confederation in particular, by replacing that confederation with a government. *The Federalist Papers* delineate the character of that republican solution.[31]

In his chapter on the Civil War, Boorstin understands or interprets Lincoln's opposition to slavery in terms of its contemplated effect on the white population. More precisely, he states that the "half slave, half free" aphorism in Lincoln's speeches was simply another way of saying that the labor of

Blacks would drive free northern workingmen out of their jobs.[32] The half slave, half free aphorism in Lincoln meant exactly what it said; i.e., that this nation could not continue to exist half slave and half free, at least not if it were going to remain a democratic nation. On the other hand, if democracy, as Boorstin later states, is merely the mechanism of majority consent, then majorities have the right, as Senator Douglas claimed, to vote slavery up or down; and nations which are half slave and half free are entitled to call themselves democratic. But even here there is a real problem; for, as Lincoln indicated, once majorities begin to discriminate against certain minorities, what is to prevent that process of discrimination from culminating in minority rule and ultimately in tyranny. When Douglas argued that the inhabitants of a free territory had the God-given right to determine for themselves whether they would live in slave states or free states, he clearly implied, whether he meant it or not, that this nation *could* exist half slave and half free. In fact, he really believed that slavery had no future in the states made out of the Western territories. Still, the fact remains that Douglas was espousing a doctrine that, in Lincoln's judgment, constituted a serious backsliding from the democratic tradition established by the Founding Fathers. And as Boorstin himself admits, Lincoln, in nearly every one of his principal speeches, appealed to the *authentic* revolutionary tradition, that is, to the political theory of the Founding Fathers as he understood it.[33] But that appeal was not, as Boorstin believes, based on the contemplated effect of slavery on the jobs of free white workingmen.

In still another place, Boorstin observes that in Lincoln's understanding "the Union"—and not any self-conscious culture—was what needed to be preserved.[34] It is true that Lincoln wrote to Horace Greeley that his "paramount object" in the Civil War was to "save" the Union, and that if he could save it without freeing any slave he would do it, or if by freeing all the slaves he would do that. Whatever I do about slavery, Lincoln said, I do because I believe it helps to save the Union.[35] But Lincoln made it perfectly clear (although not in this particular letter) that the Union and the Constitution were the "picture of silver" framed around the "apple of gold." And without the latter, which is the principle of "liberty to all," we could not have secured our free government and consequent prosperity. As Lincoln explained it: "The picture was made, not to *conceal*, or *destroy* the apple; but to *adorn*, and *preserve* it. The *picture* was made for the apple—*not* the apple for the picture."[36] If the Union was what needed to be preserved, it was to give strength and embodiment to the republican principle.

One would have thought that Boorstin would not have associated himself with "the Lincolnian view" from his discussion of Lincoln in the Civil War chapter. But in his concluding chapter, he gives full prominence to Lincoln's hatred of slavery everywhere, combined with a doubt of his own (that is, Lincoln's) capacity to make a perfect world. Boorstin has this to say: "We have, of course, our modern abolitionists, those who believe that the abolition of slavery in Russia is the sole issue in the world. . . . Some of them would seem almost as willing as Garrison to burn the Constitution in order to attain their admirable objective. There are others who take a more practical Lincolnian view. Like Lincoln, these people hate slavery everywhere, but they doubt their capacity to make a perfect world. Their main concern is to preserve and improve free institutions where they now exist."[37] There was never any question in Lincoln's mind about making a perfect world the immediate basis for political action, but at the same time he never doubted that the freedom of some men is always threatened by the fact that every other man is not entitled to equal freedom. As he asked Senator Douglas in an 1858 speech: "I should like to know if taking this old Declaration of Independence, which declares that all men are equal upon principle, and making exceptions to it, where it will stop? If one man says that it does not mean a negro, why may not another say it does not mean some other man?"[38] Boorstin states that "whatever theoretical debate went on [in the period prior to the Civil War] was concerned not with the nature of governments but rather with the nature of this particular government," whether this government is to remain "half slave and half free," without concerning itself with "the nature of governments" as such.

Boorstin cites a passage from one of Roosevelt's 1932 campaign speeches to advance the proposition that virtually a new society was brought into being in America in the stark absence of theory. The passage reads: "The country needs and, unless I mistake its temper, the country demands bold, persistent experimentation. It is common sense to take a method and try it: if it fails, admit it frankly and try another."[39] The last sentence in this same paragraph, which is omitted by Boorstin, reads: "The millions who are in want will not stand by silently forever while the things to satisfy their needs are within their reach." In the paragraph following the one just quoted from, Roosevelt continues: "We need to correct by drastic means if necessary the faults in our economic system from which we now suffer."[40] In other words, the country needs, and if its temper is correctly interpreted, *demands*, "bold, persistent experimentation" because "the millions who are in want" will not stand by "silently forever" while the things to satisfy their needs are "within their reach." The clear implication here is that mounting class discontents threaten the overthrow of our democratic system, and that therefore we need to correct the faults in our economic system by "drastic means." If one method does not work, we had better quickly try another. As Roosevelt later reviewed the situation in the opening speech of his second presidential campaign: "In the spring of 1933 we faced a crisis . . . made to order for all those who would overthrow our form of government," and we faced that crisis "with emergency action."[41] Of course Roosevelt experimented. He was dealing with circumstances, and circumstances can rarely be approached with plans or blueprints. We do not exaggerate when we say that the capitalistic economic system had come close to self-destruction in the Great Depression. Hence the central problem for Roosevelt was the restoration of a sick economy; and the great series of economic measures, by which the government assumed responsibility for the management of the economy, surely required considerable experimentation. But the political intention of those measures was to demonstrate the viability of liberal democratic institutions in a period of crisis and, by virtue of this very fact, Roosevelt recognizes a standard. One would have to grasp the character of the crisis as it was understood by Roosevelt, and in addition one would have to reconstruct his educated guesses as to how much he dared try to do. Only then could one properly grasp the relationship between experiment and intention and only then could one fairly state what Roosevelt's standards were.

There is relatively little disagreement over ends in our democratic society, says Boorstin, so the proper role for the statesman is one of conservation and reform rather than invention. He also says that a "wholesome" conservatism rests on knowledge of what is peculiarly "valuable" in the things to be conserved. Therefore the practical decision as to whether conservation is needed or not must be made in terms of some understanding of what is peculiarly valuable, or more precisely, in terms of what is the essential character of the good society. But Boorstin has no conception of what is peculiarly valuable about democracy. Therefore there is really nothing worth conserving other than the process itself, which, as we have seen, can degenerate to the point of allowing majorities to enslave minorities.

Boorstin opposes a "decent, free and God-fearing society" to "the characteristic tyrannies of our age" and is therefore concerned about the opposition between freedom and tyranny. He is opposed to loyalty oaths and heresy hunts and "dogmatic nationalism" because all these constitute a threat to the common-law liberties of the citizen, that is, a narrow definition of treason, due process of law, freedom from attainder, the rights of free speech and assembly, and so on. And Boorstin does well to quote Burke on freedom, for more than any other statesman, Burke understood that freedom must be limited in order to be preserved. His strictures against the French Revolution serve as a constant reminder that an unlimited or unconnected freedom, that is, a liberty *unconnected* with justice, is the greatest of all possible evils.[42] But Boorstin never makes the connection that Burke makes between liberty and justice. Whatever he might have in common with Burke, we can be reasonably certain that it has nothing to do with Burke's understanding of the *just* limits of freedom. Boorstin is apparently aware that there are such things as ill-conducted democracies, but he fails to understand what is implied in that awareness, for he tends to place too much reliance upon what he calls "history." But history is everything that has happened both right and wrong. It cannot judge, but must be judged. It would seem therefore that some standard must be applied to history. Otherwise the opposition between freedom and despotism is a meaningless thing.

The intent of this book, as it is stated by the author, is to help us "understand the place of theory in American political life."[43] Boorstin states that this book adds up to the warning that we cannot rely on a "philosophy of democracy" as a weapon in the "world-wide struggle against communism."[44]

Presumably discussions over national purpose frighten him. In very recent times, he says, we have heard more and more voices asking for a "democratic faith" or a philosophy of democracy, and this is not a good thing because precise definitions, or the need for "precise definitions, are more often the end than the beginning of agreement."[45] Boorstin holds that a free and therefore a good society implies "a competition among values" and not an agreement in values, and that freedom is only *valuable* to the extent that it allows this "competition" among values. It seems that the basic problem for Boorstin is that of how a democratic statesman can conserve his society—he speaks of perpetuating "the virtues of our political thought," but in order to perpetuate a virtue we would already have to know what that virtue is.[46] And what are the virtues of our political thought for Boorstin—certainly not freedom, because freedom, as he states, affirms a value only to allow a competition among values. Lincoln was able to make such a different judgment because he believed that the basic assumption of American democracy was not what Boorstin had described it to be. The freedom of some men, as he stated, is always threatened by the fact that every other man is not entitled to *equal* freedom.[47] And this awareness is the absolutely essential condition of the democratic political process; for, in our understanding, the principle of majority rule cannot be separated from the principle of the natural equality of political right of all men.

Notes and References

Chapter One

1. Samuel I. Rosenman, *Working with Roosevelt* (New York, 1952), p. 176.

2. FDR to Norman Thomas, July 31, 1940, President's Personal File 4840, Roosevelt Papers, Franklin D. Roosevelt Library, Hyde Park, New York.

3. "Tolstoy" Conference, *"Operational" Papers* (PREM 3/434/2), Public Record Office, London, 1973. The class of documents entitled *"Operational" Papers* is referred to as the Churchill Papers.

Chapter Two

1. Raymond Moley, *The First New Deal* (New York, 1966), p. xviii.

2. Remarks made at a seminar on the 1930's at Claremont Men's College in Claremont, California, on February 23, 1966.

3. Franklin D. Roosevelt, *The Public Papers and Addresses of Franklin D. Roosevelt*, compiled by S. I. Rosenman (13 vols.; New York, 1938–50), VII, 587. Hereafter referred to as *Public Papers and Addresses*.

4. Richard Hofstadter, *The American Political Tradition* (New York, 1948), p. vii.

5. *Public Papers and Addresses*, VII, 259.

6. *Ibid.*, 520.

7. *Ibid.*, 419.

8. *Ibid.*, V, 389.

9. Max Freedman, annotator, *Roosevelt and Frankfurter* (Boston: 1967), p. 381.

Chapter Three

1. *Public Papers and Addresses*, V, 579.
2. John Locke, *Second Treatise of Government*, chap. 6, para. 57.
3. *Public Papers and Addresses*, I, 755.
4. Quoted in Alpheus T. Mason, *Security through Freedom* (Ithaca, New York, 1955), p. 77.
5. *Public Papers and Addresses*, I, 754.
6. *Ibid.*, VI, 366.
7. *Ibid.*, V, 233, 234.
8. *Ibid.*, IV, 338–39, 341.
9. *Ibid.*, I, 749.
10. *Ibid.*, II, 186; III, 288; IX, 596.
11. *Ibid.*, IV, 489–90.
12. *Ibid.*, IX, 596.
13. *Ibid.*, V, 685.
14. *Ibid.*, VI, 210–11.
15. Walter Bagehot, *The English Constitution* (New York, 1961), p. 18.
16. *Public Papers and Addresses*, II, 12; V, 233–34.
17. Raymond Moley, *After Seven Years* (New York, 1939), p. 400.
18. Winston Churchill, *Great Contemporaries* (London, 1937), p. 306.
19. *Hearings before the Senate Committee on Education and Labor on S. 2926*, 73d Cong., 2d sess., Part 2, March 27, 1934, p. 407.
20. *NLRB* v. *Jones and Laughlin Steel Corp.*, 201 U.S. 1 at 42 (1937).
21. *Cong. Rec.*, 73d Cong., 2d sess., Vol. 58, Pt. 11, June 16, 1934, p. 12018.
22. Churchill, *op. cit.*, pp. 305–06.
23. Here I am heavily indebted to Professor Martin Diamond's analysis of the Madisonian view of the class struggle in his "Democracy and the Federalist: A Reconsideration of the Framers' Intent," *American Political Science Review* (March, 1959), and in his "The Federalist," *History of Political Philosophy*, ed. by Leo Strauss and Joseph Cropsey (Chicago, 1963).
24. *Public Papers and Addresses*, V, 338–39.
25. *Ibid.*, IV, 17.
26. "Social Control vs. the Constitution," *New Republic* (June 12, 1935), p. 118.
27. *Public Papers and Addresses*, VII, 9–10.

Chapter Four

1. Hofstadter, *op. cit.*, p. vii.
2. *Ibid.*, p. x.
3. *Ibid.*, p. vii.
4. *Ibid.*, p. x.
5. *Ibid.*, p. 317.
6. *Ibid.*, pp. 315–16.
7. *Ibid.*, pp. x, xi.
8. *Ibid.*, pp. x, 315.
9. *Ibid.*, p. 340.
10. *Ibid.*, p. vi.
11. *Ibid.*, p. 7.
12. *Ibid.*, p. 10.
13. *Federalist* essay 63.
14. *Federalist* essay 62.
15. Hofstadter, *op. cit.*, p. 5.
16. *Ibid.*, pp. 352, 324.
17. *Ibid.*, pp. 341–42.
18. *Public Papers and Addresses*, IV, 101.
19. Hofstadter, *The Age of Reform* (New York, 1956), p. 309n.
20. *New York Times*, February 28, 1937, p. 33.
21. Hofstadter, *The American Political Tradition*, p. 337.
22. Rexford G. Tugwell, "The Progressive Orthodoxy of Franklin D. Roosevelt," *Ethics* (October, 1953), p. 18.
23. Tugwell, *The Democratic Roosevelt* (New York, 1957), p. 349.
24. *Public Papers and Addresses*, IX, 1.
25. *Ibid.*, VII, 242.
26. *Ibid.*, V, 387.
27. *Ibid.*, VI, lxiii.
28. Elliot Roosevelt, ed., *FDR: His Personal Letters, 1928–45* (2 vols.; New York, 1950), I, 625.
29. *Public Papers and Addresses*, V, 685.
30. Hofstadter, *The American Political Tradition*, pp. vii, ix.
31. *Ibid.*, pp. 317, 351.
32. Basil Rauch, ed., *Franklin D. Roosevelt: Selected Speeches, Messages, Press Conferences and Letters* (New York, 1957), p. 37.
33. *Public Papers and Addresses*, 1, 631.
34. Hofstadter, *The American Political Tradition*, p. v.
35. John Dos Passos, *The Ground We Stand On* (New York, 1941), p. 3.
36. *Ibid.*, p. 13.
37. *Ibid.*, p. 8.
38. Hofstadter, *The American Political Tradition*, pp. vii, 324, 352.
39. Dos Passos, *op. cit.*, pp. 11, 12.

40. *Ibid.*, p. 3.
41. *Ibid.*, p. 11.
42. Hofstadter, *The American Political Tradition*, p. v.
43. Dos Passos, *op. cit.*, p. 3.

Chapter Five

1. Roosevelt, Press Conference #209, May 31, 1935, *Press Conferences of Franklin D. Roosevelt* (Hyde Park, New York, 1956), V, 322–23.
2. Quoted in Arthur M. Schlesinger, Jr., *The Politics of Upheaval* (Boston, 1960), p. 280.
3. Quoted in Arthur Lief, *The Brandeis Guide to the Modern World* (Boston, 1941), p. 70.
4. Quoted in Alexander M. Bickel, *The Unpublished Opinions of Justice Brandeis* (Chicago, 1967), pp. 119–20.
5. *A.L.A. Schechter Poultry Corp.* v. *United States*, 295 U.S. 495, 513 (1935).
6. *Ibid.* at 549.
7. *Ibid.* at 546, 548.
8. *Ibid.* at 548. Emphasis added.
9. *Ibid.* at 549–50.
10. *Public Papers and Addresses*, IV, 124. Emphasis added.
11. See *Railroad Retirement Board* v. *Alton R.R.*, 295 U.S. 330 (1935) and *Carter* v. *Carter Coal Co.*, 298 U.S. 238 (1936).
12. *NLRB* v. *Jones and Laughlin Steel Co.*, 301 U.S. 1, 76 (1937).
13. 295 U.S. 554–55.
14. *Public Papers and Addresses*, VI, lviii.
15. Rexford G. Tugwell, *The Democratic Roosevelt*, p. 385.
16. On March 29, 1937, the Supreme Court upheld the Minimum Wage Act of the State of Washington; on April 12, the National Labor Relations Act was upheld; and on May 24, the Social Security Act was similarly upheld.
17. Statement of Robert H. Jackson, *Hearings before the Senate Judiciary Committee on S. 1392*, 75th Cong., 1st sess., Part 1, March 11, 1937.
18. Merlo J. Pusey, *Charles Evans Hughes* (2 vols.; New York: 1951), II, 755.
19. *Ibid.*, 788.

Chapter Six

1. There was no roll-call in the Senate on the final version of the

wages and hours bill agreed to on June 24, 1938 (which agreement was produced by a conference committee). Anyway, the most important compromises had already been made with the South and incorporated into the final version of the bill before it was voted on. Consequently, the roll-call vote on the earlier version of the bill is more revealing of the opposition Democrats' attitude toward that piece of legislation.

2. Although the President was not able to include the Virginia senators, Glass and Byrd, in his "purge" attempts (for neither was up for reelection in 1938), he did initiate maneuvers around that time to hand over the federal patronage in Virginia to its governor, contrary to established custom. The next year, in February, 1939, he nominated Floyd H. Roberts as district judge for the western district of Virginia in the face of objections from the Virginia senators, and the Senate voted 72 to 9 to refuse to give its consent to the nomination. Senator Byrd suggested that Roberts's nomination was related to the purge of the previous year: "The purpose of the President to recognize other political personages in Virginia as to appointments on which the Senators have the constitutional duty of confirmation was publicly announced coincident with the 'purge' efforts last Spring. . . . This appointment has been made a vehicle to carry out the political purpose of retaliation" (*New York Times*, February 10, 1939, p. 14).

3. *Public Papers and Addresses*, VII, 467–68.

4. *New York Times*, August 12, 1938, p. 16.

5. *Ibid.*, September 25, 1938, IV, 7.

6. *Public Papers and Addresses*, VII, 469–70. Emphasis added.

7. The editorial cites thirteen administration bills that the senator supported and four that he opposed during the 1935–1936 period. Out of this group, however, he supported only three important New Deal measures—the Wagner labor relations bill, the Social Security bill, and the tax-the-wealth bill—and opposed the same number—the public utility holding company control bill, the Guffey-Snyder coal bill, and the Wagner-Ellenbogen housing bill.

8. FDR to Mrs. Mabel Walker Willebrandt, September 8, 1938, President's Personal File 1986, Roosevelt Papers, Franklin D. Roosevelt Library, Hyde Park, New York. See Anne O'Hare McCormick, "As He Sees Himself," *New York Times Magazine*, October 16, 1938, VIII, 1.

9. *Public Papers and Addresses*, IX, 28.

10. James Farley, *Jim Farley's Story* (New York, 1948), pp. 146–47.

11. See, for example, Basil Rauch, *The History of The New Deal, 1933–38* (New York, 1944), chap. 14; Richard Hofstadter, *The American Political Tradition*, chap. 12; James MacGregor Burns, *Roosevelt: The Lion and the Fox* (New York, 1956), chap. 18, and *The Deadlock of Democracy* (Englewood Cliffs, N.J., 1963), chap. 7; Rexford G. Tugwell, *The Democratic Roosevelt*, chap. 22; and William E.

Leuchlenburg, *Franklin D. Roosevelt and the New Deal, 1932–1940* (Chicago, 1963), chap. 11.

12. Roosevelt, *Public Papers of* [*Governor*] *Franklin D. Roosevelt, 1932* (Albany, New York, 1939), p. 664.

13. *Public Papers and Addresses*, III, 436; V, 148.

14. *Ibid.*, VII, 453. The italics are mine.

Chapter Seven

1. Edward J. Flynn, *You're the Boss* (New York, 1947), p. 229.

2. *Public Papers and Addresses*, VI, 114–15.

3. Joseph Alsop and Turner Catledge, *The 168 Days* (New York, 1938), p. 204.

4. Farley, *op. cit.*, p. 151.

5. Quoted in Grace Tully, *FDR, My Boss* (New York, 1949), p. 180.

6. Bascom N. Timmons, *Garner of Texas* (New York, 1948), p. 259.

7. S. K. Padover, ed., *The Washington Papers* (New York, 1955), p. 247.

8. *Ibid.*, p. 216.

9. *Ibid.*, pp. 220–21.

10. *Ibid.*, pp. 224–25.

11. *Ibid.*, p. 220.

12. *Public Papers and Addresses*, VIII, 208.

13. Frances Perkins, *The Roosevelt I Knew* (New York, 1946), p. 126.

14. Eleanor Roosevelt, *This I Remember* (New York, 1949), pp. 217–18.

15. Farley, *op. cit.*, p. 293.

16. *Public Papers and Addresses*, VII, 7, 12.

17. *New York Times*, July 15, 1940, p. 14.

18. *Federalist* essay 72.

Chapter Eight

1. John Toland, "Death Watch in the Pacific," *Look* magazine, September 12, 1961, p. 87.

2. Henry L. Stimson and McGeorge Bundy, *On Active Service in War and Peace* (New York, 1949), p. 610.

3. Winston Churchill, *Triumph and Tragedy* (New York, 1953), p. 335.

4. Anthony Eden, *The Reckoning* (Boston, 1965), p. 594.

5. William C. Bullitt, "A Report to the American People on China," *Life*, October 14, 1947, p. 36.

6. *Hearings before the Committee on Armed Services and the Committee on Foreign Relations, United States Senate* (Washington, 1951), Pt. 4, p. 2829.

7. Chester Wilmot, *The Struggle for Europe* (New York, 1952), p. 651.

8. Churchill, *Closing the Ring* (New York, 1951), pp. 326–27.

9. Sumner Welles, *Seven Decisions that Shaped History* (New York, 1950), p. 153.

10. George F. Kennan, *Russia and the West under Lenin and Stalin* (New York, 1962), p. 356.

11. Wilmot, *op. cit.*, p. 654.

12. Churchill, *Triumph and Tragedy*, p. 202.

13. *Ibid.*, p. 362.

14. *Public Papers and Addresses*, XIII, 498.

15. Speech in the House of Commons, February 22, 1944, *The Dawn of Liberation, War Speeches by the Rt. Hon. Winston Churchill*, Charles Eade, comp. (Boston, 1945), p. 26.

16. Department of State, *Foreign Relations of the United States, The Conferences of Malta and Yalta, 1945* (Washington, 1955) p. 203; Stanislaw Mikolajczyk, *The Rape of Poland* (New York, 1948), pp. 94–98; and Jan Ciechanowski, *Defeat in Victory* (Garden City, New York, 1947), pp. 328–34.

17. Department of State, *op. cit.*, pp. 678, 953.

18. Speech to the House of Commons, October 27, 1944, *Dawn of Liberation*, p. 288.

19. Department of State, *op. cit.*, p. 508.

20. Churchill, *Triumph and Tragedy*, pp. 343–44.

21. *Ibid.*, p. 362.

22. Department of State, *op. cit.*, p. 844.

23. Welles, *op. cit.*, pp. 150–51.

24. Department of State, *op. cit.*, p. 872.

25. Quoted in Elliott Roosevelt, *As He Saw It* (New York, 1946), p. 74.

26. *Ibid.*, p. 37.

27. *Public Papers and Addresses*, VI, 292.

28. *Ibid.*, XIII, 501.

29. The Far Eastern agreement promised to internationalize one Manchurian port and create a Russian naval base out of another. It also promised joint Russian ownership of all railways in Manchuria.

30. Department of State, *op. cit.*, pp. 669–70.

Chapter Nine

1. *Cong. Rec.*, 75th Cong., 1st sess., Vol. 81, Pt. 7, August 4, 1937, p. 8194.
2. *Ibid.*, August 5, 1937, p. 8266.
3. Roosevelt said that "the United States Government does not remain indifferent to the common life of the American citizens simply because they happen to be found in what we call 'cities.' The sanitation, the education, the housing, the working and living conditions, the economic security—in brief, the general welfare of all—are *American* concerns, insofar as they are within the range of Federal power and responsibility under the constitution" (*Public Papers and Addresses*, VI, 368–69, emphasis added.)
4. See *Report to the President on Economic Conditions in the South* (Washington, 1938).
5. *Cong. Rec.*, 75th Cong., 1st sess., Vol. 81, Pt. 7, July 29, 1937, pp. 778–89.
6. *Cong. Rec.*, 75th Cong., 3rd sess., Vol. 83, Pt. 4, March 28, 1938, p. 4194. Emphasis added.
7. Robert E. Sherwood, *Roosevelt and Hopkins* (New York, 1948), p. 211.
8. Centralization refers to the concentration of power in the national government at the expense of state and local governments; and bureaucracy, as it was understood by the earlier liberalism, means the further concentration of power in and the excessive growth of the administrative or executive branch of the government.
9. *Public Papers and Addresses*, VI, 350.
10. Thomas Paine, *The Rights of Man*, Part II, chapter 1. Emphasis added.
11. By "luxury," Roosevelt meant "comfort."
12. *Public Papers and Addresses*, I, 747. Emphasis added.
13. *Ibid.*, IX, 440. Emphasis added.
14. *Ibid.*, IV, 422.
15. *Cong. Rec.*, 75th Cong. 1st sess., Vol. 79, Pt. 8, May 29, 1935, pp. 7795, 7797.
16. *Public Papers and Addresses*, VI, 2.
17. *Ibid.*, VI, lxi.
18. *Cong. Rec.*, 74th Cong., 1st sess., Vol. 79, Pt. 8, May 29, 1935, pp. 8399–8400.
19. See Norman Thomas, *America's Way Out: A Program for Democracy* (New York, 1931), p. 131: "There is a kind of American progressivism which calls itself practical because it has no general principles. It believes in doing the next thing without enough sense of direction to know what the next thing is. Often it is retrogressive

rather than progressive in that it desires not a democratic control of machinery for the common good but a return to a simpler time when the individual had a better chance to get his own farm or start his own business. Consciously or subconsciously it finds virtue in little business against big, though little business has very often all the faults and more of the wastes of a competitive profit system than big enterprises."

20. Basil Rauch, *The History of the New Deal*, pp. ix, x.

21. See FDR's remark to the Congress in 1937 that, in his opinion, the NRA's difficulties "arose from the fact that it tried to do too much. For example, it was unwise to expect the same agency to regulate the length of working hours, minimum wages, child labor and collective bargaining on the one hand and the complicated questions of unfair trade practices and business controls on the other" (*Public Papers and Addresses*, V, 638).

22. *Public Papers and Addresses*, I, 782. Emphasis added.

23. Collective bargaining rights can still be classified as a condition of happiness, but wage and hour guarantees, Social Security benefits, and living in better residences and neighborhoods are a *part* of material happiness or well-being, as well as being the conditions of other happinesses.

24. *Steward Machine Co.* v. *Davis*, 301 U.S. 548 (1937).

25. *Public Papers and Addresses*, VII, 14. Emphasis added.

26. In a message to the Congress reviewing the broad objectives and accomplishments of his first year in office, Roosevelt suggested that well-being consisted of "security for the individual and for the family" (*ibid.*, III, 288). About a year later, in a special press conference for newspaper editors, he defined that term more broadly to include "more of the good things of life," a greater distribution of wealth in the broader sense of the word, "places to go in the summertime—recreation," assurance that one is not going to starve in his old age, and "a chance to earn a living" (*ibid.*, IV, 236–37).

Chapter Ten

1. Quoted in Robert E. Sherwood, *Roosevelt and Hopkins*, p. 73.

2. Adolph A. Berle, Jr., "Intellectuals and New Deals," *New Republic* (March 7, 1964), p. 21.

Appendix One

1. Hofstadter, *The American Political Tradition*, p. vi. Emphasis added.

2. *Ibid.*, p. viii. In his latest book, *The Progressive Historians* (New York, 1970), Hofstadter admits that his distinction between a democracy of cupidity and a democracy of fraternity, made in *The American Political Tradition*, had its source in the Marxism of the 1930's. See p. 452n.
3. Hofstadter, *The American Political Tradition*, p. x. Emphasis added.
4. *Ibid.*, p. vii.
5. *Ibid.*, p. 17.
6. *Ibid.*, p. viii.
7. *Ibid.*, pp. 16–17.
8. *Ibid.*, pp. 9–10.
9. *Ibid.*, pp. 16–17.
10. *Ibid.*, pp. 138, 139, 140.
11. *Ibid.*, pp. 149–50.
12. *Ibid.*, pp. 336–39.
13. *Ibid.*, p. 335.
14. *Ibid.*, p. 341. What Hofstadter tries to do, as becomes clear from his argument, is to suggest that Roosevelt should have moved further in the direction of socialism (that is, he should have led America into a collectivistic economy, as Rexford G. Tugwell had been pressing for).
15. *Ibid.*, p. vi.
16. Harry V. Jaffa, *Crisis of the House Divided* (New York, 1955), p. 324.
17. Hofstadter, *The American Political Tradition*, pp. 3, 16.
18. David Hawke, "Interview: Richard Hofstadter," *History* 3 (September, 1960), p. 139.
19. Hofstadter, *The American Political Tradition*, p. 137.
20. V. I. Lenin, *State and Revolution*, chapter 1.

Appendix Two

1. Edmund Burke, *The Works of the Right Honorable Edmund Burke* (12 vols.; Boston, 1881), IV, 207.
2. Daniel J. Boorstin, *The Genius of American Politics* (Chicago, 1953).
3. *Ibid.*, pp. 77, 84.
4. *Ibid.*, p. 68.
5. *Ibid.*, pp. 77, 78, 79.
6. *Ibid.*, p. 74.
7. *Ibid.*, pp. 72, 76.
8. *Ibid.*, p. 74.
9. *Ibid.*, pp. 76, 77.

10. Alexander Hamilton, *The Mind of Alexander Hamilton*, ed. by S. K. Padover (New York, 1958), p. 92.

11. Thomas Paine, *Thomas Paine, Representative Selections*, ed. by H. H. Clark (New York, 1961), pp. 112, 175, 232.

12. Boorstin, *op. cit.*, p. 76.

13. *Ibid.*

14. John Locke, *Second Treatise of Government*, chapter 2, para. 4.

15. Boorstin, *op. cit.*, pp. 126–27.

16. *Dred Scott* v. *Sanford*, 19 *How*. 393 at 406–10 (1856).

17. *Ibid.*, at 572–73.

18. Abraham Lincoln, *The Collected Works of Abraham Lincoln*, ed. by Roy P. Basler (9 vols.; New Brunswick, New Jersey, 1953), II, 405–06.

19. Jefferson himself associated the Declaration with "the elementary books of public right" written by Aristotle, Cicero, Locke, Sydney, and others. See his Letter to Henry Lee, May 8, 1825, *The Life and Selected Writings of Thomas Jefferson*, ed. by A. Koch and W. Peden (New York, 1944), p. 719.

20. Boorstin, *op. cit.*, p. 83.

21. Lincoln, *op. cit.*, II, 499–500.

22. See chapter 14 of Jaffa, *op. cit.*, for a discussion of the universal meaning of the Declaration of Independence.

23. Boorstin, *op. cit.*, pp. 85, 72–73.

24. Lincoln, *op. cit.*, III, 376.

25. Boorstin, *op. cit.*, p. 95.

26. *Ibid.*, pp. 73–96.

27. *Ibid.*, p. 97.

28. *Ibid.*, p. 101.

29. *Ibid.*

30. *Ibid.*, p. 97.

31. See Martin Diamond, "What the Framers Meant by Federalism," *A Nation of States*, ed. by R. Goldwin (Chicago, 1963), for a discussion of the theoretical basis of the "antifederalist" position.

32. Boorstin, *op. cit.*, pp. 113–14.

33. *Ibid.*, p. 126.

34. *Ibid.*, p. 131.

35. Lincoln, *op. cit.*, V, 388.

36. *Ibid.*, IV, 168–69. See Jaffa, *op. cit.*, chapter 15.

37. Boorstin, *op. cit.*, p. 188.

38. Lincoln, *op. cit.*, II, 500.

39. Boorstin, *op. cit.*, p. 119.

40. *Public Papers and Addresses*, I, 646.

41. *Ibid.*, V, 385.

42. Burke, *op. cit.*, II, 416.

43. Boorstin, *op. cit.*, p. 36.
44. *Ibid.*, p. 4.
45. *Ibid.*, pp. 168–69.
46. *Ibid.*, pp. 188–89.
47. See Jaffa, *op. cit.*, chapter 17.

Bibliography

Published Documents and Letters of FDR

ROOSEVELT, FRANKLIN D. *The Public Papers of* [*Governor*] *Franklin D. Roosevelt*. 4 vols. Albany, New York: J. B. Lyon, 1930, 1931, 1937, 1939.

———. *The Public Papers and Addresses of Franklin D. Roosevelt*. S. I. Rosenman, comp. 13 vols. New York: Random House, 1938; Macmillam, 1941; Harper, 1950.

———. *F.D.R.: His Personal Letters*. Elliott Roosevelt, ed. 4 vols. New York: Duell, Sloan and Pearce, 1947–50.

———. *Press Conferences of Franklin D. Roosevelt*. 25 vols. (microfilm). Hyde Park, New York: Franklin D. Roosevelt Library, 1956–57.

Public Documents

United States Department of State. *Foreign Relations of the United States, The Conferences of Malta and Yalta, 1945*. Washington: United States Government Printing Office, 1955.

———. *Foreign Relations of the United States, The Conferences of Cairo and Teheran, 1943*. Washington: United States Government Printing Office, 1967.

Report to the President on Economic Conditions in the South. Washington: United States Government Printing Office, 1938.

The Roosevelt Papers are divided into the President's Personal File, the President's Secretary's File, and the Official File at the Franklin D. Roosevelt Library in Hyde Park, New York.

Memoirs, Autobiographies, Observations

ALSOP, JOSEPH, and TURNER, CATLEDGE. *The 168 Days.* Garden City, New York: Doubleday, Doran, 1938.

BOHLEN, CHARLES E. *Witness to History, 1929–1969.* New York: W. W. Norton, 1973.

BULLITT, GEORGE, ed. *For the President, Personal and Secret: Correspondence between Franklin D. Roosevelt and William C. Bullitt.* Boston: Houghton Mifflin, 1972.

CHURCHILL, WINSTON. *Great Contemporaries.* London: Collins, 1937.

———. *Closing the Ring.* New York: Houghton Mifflin, 1951.

———. *Triumph and Tragedy.* New York: Houghton Mifflin, 1953.

CIENCHANOWSKI, JAN. *Defeat in Victory.* Garden City, New York: Doubleday, 1947.

EDEN, ANTHONY. *The Reckoning.* Boston: Houghton Mifflin, 1965.

FARLEY, JAMES. *Jim Farley's Story.* New York: McGraw-Hill, 1948.

FLYNN, EDWARD J. *You're the Boss.* New York: Viking Press, 1947.

KENNAN, GEORGE F. *Memoirs, 1925–50.* Boston: Little, Brown, 1967.

MIKOLAJCZYK, STANISLAW. *The Rape of Poland.* New York: Whittlesey House, 1948.

MOLEY, RAYMOND. *After Seven Years.* New York: Harper, 1939.

———. *The First New Deal.* New York: Harcourt, Brace and World, 1966.

PERKINS, FRANCES. *The Roosevelt I Knew.* New York: Viking Press, 1946.

ROOSEVELT, ELEANOR. *This I Remember.* New York: Harper, 1949.

ROOSEVELT, ELLIOTT. *As He Saw It.* New York: Duell, Sloan and Pearce, 1946.

ROSENMAN, SAMUEL I. *Working with Roosevelt.* New York: Harper, 1952.

SHERWOOD, ROBERT E. *Roosevelt and Hopkins: An Intimate History.* New York: Harper, 1948.

THOMAS, NORMAN. *America's Way Out: A Program for Democracy.* New York: Macmillan, 1931.

TIMMONS, BASCOM N. *Garner of Texas.* New York: Harper, 1948.

TUGWELL, REXFORD G. *The Democratic Roosevelt.* New York: Doubleday, 1957.

———. *The Brains Trust.* New York: Viking, 1968.

———. *How They Became President.* New York: Simon and Schuster, 1968.

TULLY, GRACE. *FDR, My Boss.* New York: Scribner's, 1949.

STIMSON, HENRY L., and MCGEORGE BUNDY. *On Active Service in War and Peace.* New York: Harper, 1949.

WELLES, SUMNER. *Seven Decisions that Shaped History.* New York: Harper, 1950.

Selected Writings

BICKEL, ALEXANDER H. *The Unpublished Opinions of Justice Brandeis.* Chicago: University of Chicago Press, 1967.

CLARK, H.H., ed. *Thomas Paine, Representative Selections.* New York: Hill and Wang, 1961.

EADE, CHARLES, comp. *The Dawn of Liberation: War Speeches by the Rt. Hon. Winston Churchill.* Boston: Little, Brown, 1945.

KOCH, ADRIENNE, and WILLIAM, PEDEN, eds. *The Life and Selected Writings of Thomas Jefferson.* New York: Random House, 1944.

LIEF, ARTHUR, ed. *The Brandeis Guide to the Modern World.* Boston: Little, Brown, 1941.

PADOVER, SAUL K., ed. *The Washington Papers.* New York: Harper, 1955.

———, ed. *The Mind of Alexander Hamilton.* New York: Harper, 1958.

RAUCH, BASIL, ed. *Franklin D. Roosevelt: Selected Speeches, Messages, Press Conferences and Letters.* New York: Holt, Rinehart and Winston, 1955.

Secondary Sources

BARRON, GLORIA J. *Leadership in Crisis: FDR and the Path to Intervention.* Port Washington, New York: Kennikat Press, 1973.

BOORSTIN, DANIEL J. *The Genius of American Politics.* Chicago: University of Chicago Press, 1953.

BURNS, JAMES MACGREGOR. *Roosevelt: The Lion and the Fox.* New York: Harcourt, Brace, 1956.

———. *The Deadlock of Democracy.* Englewood Cliffs, N.J.: Prentice-Hall, 1963.

———. *Roosevelt: The Soldier of Freedom.* New York: Harcourt Brace Jovanovich, 1970.

CLEMENS, DIANE SHAVER. *Yalta.* New York: Oxford University Press, 1970.

DOS PASSOS, JOHN. *The Ground We Stand On.* New York: Harcourt, Brace, 1941.

FEIS, HERBERT. *Churchill-Roosevelt-Stalin.* Princeton, N.J.: Princeton University Press, 1957.

FISCHER, LOUIS. *The Road to Yalta.* New York: Harper and Row, 1972.

HOFSTADTER, RICHARD. *The American Political Tradition.* New York: Alfred A. Knopf, 1948.

———. *The Age of Reform, From Bryan to F.D.R.* New York: Alfred A. Knopf, 1955.

———. *The Progressive Historians.* New York: Alfred A. Knopf, 1970.

JAFFA, HARRY V. *Crisis of the House Divided: An Interpretation of the Issues in the Lincoln-Douglas Debates.* Garden City, New York: Doubleday, 1959.

KENNAN, GEORGE F. *American Diplomacy, 1900–50.* Chicago: University of Chicago Press, 1951.

———. *Russia and the West under Lenin and Stalin.* New York: New American Library, 1952.

LEUCHTENBURG, WILLIAM E. *Franklin D. Roosevelt and the New Deal, 1932–1940.* Chicago: University of Chicago Press, 1963.

MASON, ALPHEUS T. *Security through Freedom.* Ithaca, New York: Cornell University Press, 1955.

PERKINS, DEXTER. *The New Age of Franklin D. Roosevelt, 1932–45.* Chicago: University of Chicago Press, 1957.

RAUCH, BASIL. *Roosevelt: From Munich to Pearl Harbor.* New York: Creative Age Press, 1950.

———. *The History of the New Deal.* New York: Capricorn Books, 1963.

SCHLESINGER, ARTHUR M., JR. *The Crisis of the Old Order.* Boston: Houghton Mifflin, 1957.

———. *The Coming of the New Deal.* Boston: Houghton Mifflin, 1959.

———. *The Politics of Upheaval.* Boston: Houghton Mifflin, 1960.

WILMOT, CHESTER. *The Struggle for Europe.* New York: Harper, 1952.

Articles

BERLE, ADOLPH A., JR. "Intellectuals and New Deals." *New Republic* (March 7, 1964), 21–24.

BULLITT, WILLIAM C. "A Report to the American People on China." *Life* (October 13, 1947), 35–36, 139–40, 142, 145–46, 148, 151–52, 154.

COHEN, JACOB. "Schlesinger and the New Deal." *Dissent* (Autumn, 1961), 461–72.

CROSSMAN, R.H.S. "Towards a Philosophy of Socialism." *New Fabian Essays*, ed. by R.H.S. Crossman. New York: Frederick A. Praeger, 1952, 1–32.

DIAMOND, MARTIN. "Democracy and the Federalist: A Reconsideration of the Framers' Intent." *American Political Science Review* (March, 1959), 52–86.

———. "What the Framers Meant by Federalism." *A Nation of States*, ed. by Robert A. Goldwin. Chicago: Rand-McNally, 1963, 24–41.

———. "The Federalist." *History of Political Philosophy*, ed. by Leo Strauss and Joseph Cropsey. Chicago: Rand-McNally, 1963, 573–93.

———. "The Ends of Federalism." *Publius* (Fall, 1973), 129–52.

———. "The Problems of the Socialist Party." *Failure of a Dream*, ed. by John M. Laslett and Seymour M. Lipset. Garden City, New York: Anchor/Doubleday, 1974, 362–79.

EDITORS. "Social Control vs. the Constitution." *New Republic* (June 12, 1935), 116–18.

SCHLESINGER, ARTHUR M., JR. "Sources of the New Deal." *Paths of American Thought*, ed. by A. M. Schlesinger, Jr., and Morton White. Boston: Houghton Mifflin, 1963, 372–91.

TOLAND, JOHN. "Death Watch in the Pacific." *Look* magazine (September 12, 1961), 87–88, 191–95.

TUGWELL, REXFORD G. "The Progessive Orthodoxy of Franklin D. Roosevelt." *Ethics* (October, 1953), 1–23.

Interviews

HAWKE, DAVID. "Interview: Richard Hofstadter." *History 3* (September, 1960), 135–41.

KROCK, ARTHUR. "The President Discusses His Political Philosophy." *New York Times* (February 28, 1937), 1, 33.

MCCORMICK, ANNE O'HARE. "An Unchanging Roosevelt Drives Steadily On." *New York Times Magazine* (August 15, 1938), VIII, 1–2, 14.

———. "As He Sees Himself." *New York Times Magazine* (October 16, 1938), VII, 1–3, 19.

Other Sources

BAGEHOT, WALTER, *The English Constitution.* New York: 1961.

BURKE, EDMUND. *The Works of the Right Honorable Edmund Burke.* 12 vols. Boston: Little, Brown, 1881.

HAMILTON, ALEXANDER, and JAMES, MADISON. *The Federalist.*

LENIN, V.I. *State and Revolution.*

LINCOLN, ABRAHAM. *The Collected Works of Abraham Lincoln.* Ed. by Roy P. Basler. 9 vols. New Brunswick, New Jersey: Rutgers University Press, 1953.

LOCKE, JOHN. *Two Treatises of Government.*

PAINE, THOMAS. *The Rights of Man.*

Index